THE MYSTICAL WAY IN EVERYDAY LIFE

THE MYSTICAL WAY IN EVERYDAY LIFE
Sermons, Prayers, and Essays

Karl Rahner, S.J.

Translated, Edited, and with an Introduction by
Annemarie S. Kidder

ORBIS BOOKS
Maryknoll, New York 10545

Translation copyright © 2010 by Annemarie S. Kidder.

Texts from *Glaube, der die Erde liebt* are found in Volumes 3, 7, 10, 12, 14, 22/2 of *Karl Rahner Sämtliche Werke* © Verlag Herder GmbH, Freiburg im Breisgau and Karl Rahner, *Alltägliche Dinge* is taken from *Karl Rahner Sämtliche Werke* Volume 23 © Verlag Herder GmbH, Freiburg im Breisgau by courtesy of Deutsche Provinz der Jesuiten, München, Germany.

Published by Orbis Books, Maryknoll, NY 10545-0302.

Manufactured in the United States of America.

Library of Congress Cataloging-in-Publication Data

Rahner, Karl, 1904-1984.
  [Selections. English. 2010]
  The mystical way in everyday life : sermons, prayers, and essays / Karl Rahner; translated, edited, and with an Introduction by Annemarie S. Kidder.
    p. cm.
  Includes index.
  ISBN 978-1-57075-867-6 (pbk.)
  1. Spirituality—Catholic Church. 2. Spiritual life—Catholic Church. 3. Mysticism—Catholic Church. I. Kidder, Annemarie S. II. Title.
  BX2350.65.R3413 2010
  248.2'2—dc22
                    2009042173

CONTENTS

Lent

Easter

Corpus Christi and Pentecost

Love for God and Neighbor

The One Spirit—The Many Gifts

The Mystery of the Saints

Mysteries of Everyday Life

A Theology of Everyday Life

Words for the Start of the Day

FOREWORD

KARL CARDINAL LEHMANN

The original slim pocketbook edition of this book was published by Herder in 1966. When I became assistant to Karl Rahner on July 1, 1964, I perused all the texts of his that were unfamiliar to me and discovered a good number of shorter ones, mainly on the church year. These texts had been published in rather obscure places, and hence were virtually forgotten. Among them were many texts produced between 1948 and 1950. There were also a few shorter pieces, written in a similar style and stemming largely from the period prior to the Second Vatican Council.

When I suggested to Karl Rahner that he publish a little book with these texts, he soon gave me his full permission with regard to the selections and the suggested outline. He was always generous when it came to his associates' suggestions. His confidence gave me positive encouragement again and again.

Three reasons in particular motivated me to propose such a collection. First, I had a profound desire to show the internal unity between Rahner's simple, spiritually deep, and linguistically often beautiful texts and those texts of his that were often seen as extremely difficult and complex. Second, I wanted to object to the tendency of some of his critics who were dismissing him as a "hopeless speculator" or who were downgrading his spiritual texts as lacking any particular importance. Finally, I came up with the title "A Faith that Loves the Earth." After the council, the objection was frequently raised that the church had either made too many concessions to the secular world or was withdrawing from it into her own interiority—a fruitless criticism found among so-called conservatives and progressives, respectively, up to the present day. As I discovered, however, Rahner in his early meditations and reflections had already created an integration of faith and the world, an integration that blurred neither their distinction nor their interdependence. Here was a faith that did not flee from responsibility toward the world, nor did it assimilate to the secular world or become lost in it. For that reason, the original title of "A Faith that Loves the Earth" seemed fitting.

I am glad that the little book is still well received today. While it is good that the German edition of Rahner's *Sämtliche Werke* ("Collected Works") is advancing so well and can gather up the many fruits of Rahner's thought, it is also unfortunate that as a result one or another volume or little book that was of importance during Karl Rahner's lifetime and had been a readers' favorite should disappear. When these books and texts are presented again in their original format, as has been done on occasion over the last few years, they become a beautiful testimony to the living legacy of Karl Rahner.

For that reason, I am pleased with the publication of an American translation upon the twenty-fifth anniversary of Karl Rahner's death, and I wish this edition great success and God's blessings. I am firmly convinced that these texts are still—or, better yet, are especially today—of the greatest importance, fresh, and hence so very relevant.

Mainz, Easter 2009

INTRODUCTION

ANNEMARIE S. KIDDER

Karl Rahner, S.J., (1904–1984) has come to be regarded as one of the most influential theologians of our time. His bibliography includes more than sixteen hundred entries in German alone, spanning editorials, essays, lectures, sermons, prayers, book reviews, dictionary entries, and books on prayer, penance, the spiritual life, Ignatius of Loyola's *Exercises* and spirituality, and systematic theology. His contributions to the Second Vatican Council (1963–1965) shaped in significant ways the doctrinal formulations on the church, the sacraments, and the role of the laity in the Roman Catholic Church. And his efforts at reconciling the scholastic approach to church doctrine with an existential, transcendental, and anthropological understanding of humanity's relationship with God has earned him the reputation of having opened doors for ecumenical dialogue with those outside the church, along with having fostered a scientific worldview and an intentional engagement with the secular world. Rahner wrote on a wide range of topics and issues facing the church of his time, topics and issues pertaining to Christians and non-Christians alike.

In light of Rahner's prolific output, students are faced with a formidable and somewhat bewildering bibliographical legacy, a mountain from which choosing to quarry a rather modest portion of the whole can still become the task of a lifetime. Added to the difficulty of knowing where to begin amidst a plethora of potential starting points is Rahner's seem-ingly philosophical approach to theology, his complex and complicated sentence structure with its numerous dependent clauses and parenthetical interjections, and his tendency to presuppose among his audience at least a rudimentary knowl-edge of philosophy, theology, patristic studies, and the scholas-tic method.

A cursory perusal of Rahner's writings can lead one to con-clude that his thought is abstract, complex, and heady. Cer-tainly, Rahner studied philosophy at the University of Freiburg under the philosopher Martin Heidegger. And, even after he completed his theological studies and was appointed to a pro-fessorship in theology at the University of Innsbruck, his theo-logical essays and lectures continued to be philosophically col-ored, leading some to conclude that Rahner was more philosopher than theologian. In addition, many of his topical essays begin with the formulation of a problem, proceed in question-and-answer format toward an elaboration on the best method for approaching the problem, and imitate a philosoph-ical discourse in a type of language that sounds more spoken than written, despite its complexities. All the while, explicit re-ligious language is largely avoided and theological concepts are referenced and employed with caution or parenthetically.

Given these tendencies in methodology and language, it is not surprising that Rahner has often been studied for his method of argumentation and from the perspective of philo-sophical thought and its underpinnings rather than for his contributions to spiritual theology and the practice of the spir-itual life. "You had better know your Heidegger," is a frequent comment heard by those professing to study Rahner, as if the theological factors that influenced him—his religious order, the Society of Jesus, and its founder, Ignatius of Loyola, along with the father of scholastic theology, Thomas Aquinas, whose theological methodology was in standard use up to the time of the Second Vatican Council (hence during Rahner's formative years)—were far less significant.

The particular questions one asks of someone's work and the lens of biographical or methodological considerations through which the work is read will determine the answers obtained. In Rahner's case, the questions asked of his work today differ considerably from those asked by a previous generation. The doctrinal changes that Vatican II implemented needed further explanation, elaboration, and clarification. Since Rahner played a critical role in this regard, his essays and lectures were often read through the lens of what the Second Vatican Council's changes would mean for the future of the church and its members. More than forty years after the council's decisions and in the light of subsequent developments, however, some of these speculations, along with the hopes for far-reaching changes, have become moot. Instead, the church is now faced with the full flowering of a new situation, often referred to as the postmodern era.

The postmodern era, ushered in with the dropping of the atomic bomb and the end of World War II, denotes a shift in perceptions and priorities. People in the postmodern era have lost confidence in the idea of perpetual progress advanced by the sciences and technology. They have become distrustful of and disenchanted with authority, which includes that of the church. They value experience over against outside authority, a faith based on experience over against one that is ecclesiastically pre-formulated, and a plurality of voices that are of equal value over against a singular voice that makes all final decisions. Authenticity, being true to one's self, is more important than giving assent; personal narrative in the context of community is more important than subscribing to creedal statements. Traditional formulations of the Christian faith and the "correct" answers to faith questions, as in catechesis, have come to be ranked as having lesser importance than one's own personal creed and a first-hand knowledge of the Christian faith. The experience of worship, the celebration of the sacraments, spiritual practices, prayer, meditation, and the use of the arts all contribute to allowing for an encounter with the divine. As a result, people of the postmodern era have rediscovered the writings of the mystics and their way of praying and speaking with God, their attitudes toward the divine, their fundamental awareness of God's activity and their response to it.

It is from this vantage point that Rahner is being re-read, re-examined, and re-evaluated. Surprisingly, he is found addressing the concerns of both believers and non-believers in their quest for meaning, for a fulfilled life, for a life that finds its origin and its end in what some people call "God." Rahner's writings of more than forty or fifty years ago appear to have been penned for exactly a time like this. And readers are left with the profound impression that their own attitude toward God can still go far deeper than they had thought possible. Rahner's writings urge one to withstand the silence of a hidden and mysterious God. They stimulate the urgency in one's search for an intimate God experience. And they offer concrete guidance in how to undertake the Christian pilgrimage in everyday life.

Thoughtful Christians, regardless of denominational affiliation, and students of Rahner's theology can ill afford skipping over two seminal collections of prayers and meditations. They are *Encounters with Silence*,[1] originally published in 1938, and *On Prayer* or *The Need and the Blessing of Prayer*,[2] Lenten sermons preached in 1946 in the war-ravaged and hunger-stricken city of Munich at the Bürgersaal Church of the Marian (male) congregation, because the Jesuit church, St. Michael's in the heart of Munich, had been completely destroyed and was not rebuilt until 1953.

For years, the faithful of St. Michael's parish worshiped at the nearby Bürgersaal Church, which despite war damage was able to serve, according to a sign posted above the church entrance, as "St. Michael's Emergency Church."[3] It is against the backdrop of the war's destruction—piles of stone and rubble, pangs of hunger and lost lives or crippled limbs, disorientation and trampled values—that Rahner offers people glimpses of hope and pointers to God's self-disclosed presence in their midst. The prayers written at the height of the Nazi regime and the post-war Lenten reflections presented in the context of a devastated city and land offer an entry point to Rahner's devotional life, his relational attitude toward God, and the personal piety that marked him as a Christian, a theologian, a mystic. They offer glimpses into an encounter between the human being and God that does not appear reserved for the few but can be experienced by anyone willing to take the time to watch, to listen, and to pray. The human-divine relationship revealed in these prayerful conversations and reflections shows vulnerability and honesty, admittance of doubt and shortcomings and fears as well as unrelenting hope.

Invariably, this relationship can be characterized as mystical, demonstrating both an intimate familiarity with the conversation partner and a reverent awe, a sense of God's closeness and of God's incomprehensibility and vast grandeur. In the mystical way of seeing, ordinary life and everyday events are interpreted in light of the extraordinary, the natural from the perspective of the supernatural, the concrete from the position of the transcendent, the human from the view of the divine. Such a way of seeing becomes possible for people who permit a surrender to the silent mystery of an incomprehensible God who has made himself subject to human history and human fate, people, in short, who have the subtle sense that God can draw close, who have come to know a God who dwells among and with them, and who are willing to submit and respond to God's self-revelation and self-communication in the concrete places and times, amidst the joys and celebrations as well as the sorrowful moments of crisis and destruction, of their everyday lives.

For Rahner, all people have the capability to experience God and become mystics. Rahner calls this capability that has become historical reality through God's incarnation in Jesus Christ and is given to humans at least in principle by the Holy Spirit, the "supernatural existential," a view he may have developed as early as 1937 and that can be found also in the early church fathers.[4] But not all people are in a position to identify and name their God experience in terms of the ways it relates to the triune God, the one who chose to become manifest in human history as the Word made flesh, the divine face revealed and communicated in the human face of Jesus Christ.

To that end, Rahner invites readers to pray with him, see with him, and experience with him the encounter with what people commonly call "God" and perhaps allow for the possibility that this God may be identified as the Christ who has been revealed in scripture, worshiped by the early church and in the tradition of the patristic age, and raised up through the teachings and faith practices of Christ's body, the church.

Writings in This Collection

The selections of sermons and essays in this collection are largely from two books. They are *Glaube, der die Erde liebt* (A Faith that Loves the Earth), titled after one of the volume's sermons and published in English in 1968 as *Everyday Faith*,[5] and *Alltägliche Dinge* (Everyday Things), a brief theology of everyday life, edited by the Roman Catholic theologian Hans Küng and published originally in 1964 by Benziger. Due to their complexity of argument and length, two theological essays in *Everyday Faith* are omitted: they are "Meditation zu Neujahr" ("Meditation for the New Year") and the rather technical essay on the role of Joseph, the husband of Mary, titled "Nimm das Kind und seine Mutter!" ("Take the Child and His Mother!"), which even when first published had been extensively revised from the original.

All sermons, essays, and prayers have been newly translated. Their arrangement follows that of *Everyday Faith* as originally edited by Rahner's assistant at the time, Karl Lehmann, who is now a cardinal and head of the German bishops' conference. Other pieces are included for their pertinence to section headings and for their thematic relevance to mysticism. The added pieces are three sermons on Epiphany, Lent, and Easter; essays on theologians who were influential in forming Rahner's mysticism—two on Ignatius of Loyola and one on Thomas Aquinas; the 1964 theological reflection on the mysticism of everyday life, "Everyday Things"; and six morning meditations, also addressing a mysticism of everyday life, broadcast on Radio Innsbruck in 1955.

Rahner's View of Mysticism

For Rahner, mysticism is the possibility for humans to encounter God. It is the possibility of being grasped by this silent mystery, called God, and of perceiving God's self-communication in a direct encounter. Thus, mysticism involves the practice of contemplation, prayer, and reflection that allows one to hear and discern the divine. But it is more than that. Mysticism involves understanding and practicing, right seeing and right praying, a theology and an application. Mysticism is especially needed when people have the impression that God can no longer be discovered, that a secularized, self-sufficient, technological, and scientific age with its laws has preempted the need to search for a God who lends purpose and meaning to humanity, world history, and the evolutionary cosmic struggle. Mysticism helps recover the presence of God in the world and in everyday life; it makes intelligible the personal experience with God, unmasks false God experiences, and allows God's presence to emerge where one might have overlooked or ignored it.

All people have the capacity for a God experience. This capacity results from the nature of the human mind and the grace of divine self-communication that is always offered to everyone. In Rahner's words, "there is something like an anonymous, unthematic, perhaps repressed, basic experience of being oriented to God" in humans. This basic orientation, inherent to the human make-up, can be repressed but not destroyed and is "'mystical' or (if you prefer a more cautious terminology) has its climax in what the older teachers called infused contemplation."[6]

Mysticism is best learned from the ancient Christian masters of spirituality, from the way they practiced such contemplation and the way they prayed, sought after, and longed for God. In their relationship with God they modeled a depth of possibilities by which the silent, distant, hidden, divine mystery can be experienced, addressed, and loved. However, their perspectives were also colored by their time-conditioned situation, hence they need translating into modern language and into a "modern existential ontology" or a "modern theological anthropology."[7] Mysticism takes seriously where people are, what they fear, what they know and experience in the here and now.

When in 1970 the church declared Teresa of Avila the first woman doctor of the church, Rahner suggested that this was more than an affirmative gesture toward the role of women in the church; it was an affirmation of mysticism: "Teresa is proclaimed as a teacher of mysticism. This means first of all that a person who teaches something about mysticism is doing theology, is speaking in the light of revelation, saying something to the Church as such for the edification of the faithful."[8]

Thus, mystics have something to teach us of the "depth and radicality of the experience of God" that we could not find on our own. In fact, Teresa's use of concrete imagery makes her a particularly good interpreter of the Christian faith, since "our relationship to God today must either be mediated perhaps more explicitly than ever through our relationship to the concrete Jesus of Nazareth, to his life and death and his relationship to his fellow-men, or it will not exist at all ..."[9]

A personal experience with God in Christ is needed for an authentic, robust faith among Christians. In 1966, Rahner linked this personal experience of God with mysticism: "The devout of tomorrow will be a 'mystic,' someone who has 'experienced' something, or else he or she will not be at all."[10] Rahner was objecting to the way in which the Christian faith and Christian doctrine were being taught.

Scholastic theology had insisted that grace could not be experiential, but rather could be recognized only when given from without, as through the sacraments and the proclaimed word. Now Rahner was saying that people needed more than to learn *about* God; they needed to meet and encounter God directly and personally. To that end, he attempted to develop a theology that regarded the personal experience of grace, the so-called mystical way, as the source of revelation and of theological authority, not in contrast to the methods and arguments of scholasticism and the teachings and the sacraments of the church, but in conjunction with them and as a logical outflow, continuation, and consequence of both. By including the experience of grace as an authoritative voice in formulating the faith, Rahner could broaden the understanding of the church, the sacraments, and the meaning of the individual's everyday life.

The degree to which a mystical perspective can change traditional church teaching is well illustrated by Rahner's "revised" approach to the sacraments. In his 1974 book *Die Siebenfältige Gabe* (The Sevenfold Gift), translated into English in 1977 as *Meditations on the Sacraments*, Rahner explores the nature of the church and its sacraments. To him, Jesus Christ is the primordial sacrament (*Ursakrament*), while the church is the basic sacrament (*Grundsakrament*) and the visible and socio-historical continuation of the Christ event. The church, as the basic sacrament and sign that perpetuates Christ's presence in the world, administers the seven particular sacraments or "performs" these sacred signs to work toward and enhance the Christian's salvation. The traditional understanding of sacrament is that it functions as an isolated event that occurs in the life of the believer. Through the single act of the sacrament, "God reaches into space and time to confer grace under signs instituted by Christ." Rahner suggests a new understanding of sacrament, one that "contrasts with the traditional understanding while remaining entirely within the bounds of orthodoxy."[11] The key to his new concept of sacrament is a new understanding of grace.

For Rahner, grace does not happen only in isolated instances, such as when the sacraments are administered or during so-called grace events in the course of a person's life, when one happens to recognize and accept grace. Instead, grace is everywhere, "whether in the mode of merely preceding the act, or in the mode of acceptance, or in the mode of rejection."[12] This preceding grace and its acceptance is observed when the church pledges itself to people as the basic sacrament of salvation in word and deed and when people in turn accept this pledge and act on it. The act of the church's pledging occurs through the sacraments, while the act of people's acceptance of that grace and living it out occurs both within the church and in the world.

Thus the sacraments are "in the first place" the "ecclesial manifestations and historical incarnations of *that* grace which is at work everywhere in the history of mankind and manifests itself historically, though in highly diversified ways," including in those moments when people do good and act morally.[13] Second, the sacraments are the concrete manifestations of "that mysterious grace which inconspicuously governs our whole life"; they are "the celebration in the community of the Church of that which wills to find its victory in the monotony and pain of daily life."[14]

It makes little difference to Rahner whether one calls the experience of grace "mystical" or not. What matters is that people "understand that they have an implicit but true knowledge of God," though it may not be considered that or even be verbalized by them as such and that they can have "a genuine experience of God, which is ultimately rooted in their spiritual existence, in their transcendentality, in their personality, or whatever you want to name it."[15]

For Rahner, the experience of God is the experience of grace in everyday life. According to Harvey Egan, S.J., Rahner's entire theological enterprise can be summed up in the experience of grace, or "God's self-communication at the heart of human existence," making Rahner "the preeminent theologian of experienced grace."[16] Such grace is manifested most commonly in life's banality and in its humdrum activities, its dullness and burdensome expressions, its gray dress and repetitious cycle. In what Egan calls Rahner's "mysticism of everyday life,"[17] God can be encountered by people in the routines of work, walking, sitting down, seeing, laughing, eating, and sleeping. In fact, those who practice the mysticism of daily life are looking for "God in all things," as Ignatius taught, especially in the readily available ordinariness of their routine. Rather than seeking after extraordinary spiritual gifts and ecstasies, such as speaking in tongues and experiencing mystical visions, mystics of everyday life live out "the more excellent way" that the apostle Paul describes in 1 Corinthians 13: they practice the love of God in loving their neighbor and they find God in their humble, persevering, and self-giving service to one another.

Rahner contrasts the mysticism of everyday life with that of the canonized saints and modern-day charismatics. The saints with their extraordinary mysticism differ from other Christians not in that they have attained a more valuable God experience. Rather, they have had the natural ability for concentration, submersion into the self, self-emptying, and the suspension of their natural faculties in an unusual, though still natural manner. Their ways may teach us to enhance our meditative and contemplative faculties for a more clear and distinct experience of God in everyday life, but they should not make us wish to attain precisely what they experienced.

Charismatics in modern-day life, on the other hand, are those claiming an experience of the gifts of the Holy Spirit, manifested in dramatic faith conversions, glossolalia, faith healings, prophesy, ecstatic visions, and swooning. Rahner calls the charismatic movement a "mysticism of the masses,"[18] one that is much more common than that of the saints and can awaken the desire for prayer and the scriptures, enhance the Christian's joy, build up the Christian community, and make the experience of God more tangible and concrete.

However, the charismatic experience can also distort the perception of God, suggesting to the believer "an almost naïve immediacy to God, bordering on a naïve faith in the power of the Holy Spirit."[19] Rahner predicts that the future church will hold two types of mystics: those who are given to the mysticism of the masses and those who practice a mysticism of everyday life or what he calls "a wintry spirituality," which "is closely allied with the torment of atheists" and modern rationalism, even though those who practice it are Christians who pray, worship, and receive the sacraments.[20]

While being respectful of charismatic Christians, Rahner prefers the wintry-type of mysticism. "There is a mysticism of daily life," he says, "the finding of God in all things, the sober drunkenness of the Spirit mentioned by the Church Fathers and ancient liturgy, which we dare not reject or disdain just because it is sober."[21] This is the type of mysticism portrayed in the church fathers' writings to which Rahner had been drawn during his years of theological studies, a mysticism whose essence is found consistently throughout the church's history and tradition and whose validity and practicality Rahner sought to recover for modern and perhaps postmodern times.

Patristic Studies and Mysticism

At an early age, Rahner was drawn to religious literature and read the *Imitation of Christ* by Thomas à Kempis, particularly the fourth book, containing a reflection on the Eucharist. He also translated from Latin into German hymns by Thomas Aquinas. Rahner's theological studies at the Jesuit theologate in Valkenburg, Holland, from 1929 to 1933 led him to become, in his own words, "interested in theological questions, above all in spiritual theology, in the history of piety, in patristic mysticism, and also in Bonaventure."[22]

Rahner's interest in the Christian mysticism of the patristic age is reflected in his first significant publications while still a seminarian, dealing with Origen's and Bonaventure's notions of the spiritual senses (1932–1934) and, after graduation, his 1939 book *Aszese und Mystik in der Väterzeit* (Asceticism and Mysticism in the Patristic Era). The latter is a translation of a 1930 French book by fellow Jesuit Marcel Viller on mysticism during the first six hundred years of Christian thought and practice; the translation contains emendations, updated research, suggestions for future study, and elaborate bibliographical references tailored to a German-speaking audience by Rahner, making it nearly double the size of its French original. Painstakingly researched and worked on between 1937 and 1938, the book gives evidence of Rahner's keen grasp of such church fathers as Clement of Alexandria, Origen, Evagrius Ponticus, Gregory of Nyssa, and John Climacus, to name a few. A reviewer praised it as "the first comprehensive and reliable German work on the subject";[23] it has remained the most comprehensive and reliable German work on the subject to this day.

The mere fact that the book has not been translated into English to date confirms that Rahner's early interest in mysticism has been mostly overlooked by Rahner scholars. This is also evidenced by the fact that "the significance of the book for the entire work of Rahner's has been hardly noted and examined."[24] In retrospect, Rahner's theology gains a new dimension when read through the frame of early Christian spirituality and mysticism, monastic ideals, and early Christian liturgy and sacramental practice.

Rahner was also drawn to the mystical concept developed by the church fathers that the church had sprung from the wound in Christ's side, like the second Eve stemming from the side of the second Adam, Christ. It was on this theme, found in John 19:34, that Rahner later wrote his 1936 doctoral dissertation in theology. The dissertation, drawing heavily on the church fathers and later interpreters of the first thousand years of Christianity, was never published during Rahner's lifetime and was made available to the public only in 1999, when it was included in the third volume of Karl Rahner's *Sämtliche Werke*, on *Spiritualität und Theologie der Kirchenväter* ("Spirituality and

Theology of the Church Fathers"),[25] along with *Aszese und Mystik in der Väterzeit.*

On his own, the seminarian Rahner explored the early understanding of grace and the spiritual life through the writings of the church fathers. He also began studying early baptismal rites and liturgies, rites of Christian initiation, and the history of penance and confession, all subjects that would be of lifelong interest to him. As can be gleaned from his extensive personal reading list, during the first year of his theological education Rahner read, in addition to Augustine, almost all the sources of the second Christian century, such as the apostolic fathers Justin and Irenaeus, the Apocryphal Acts and martyr stories, the Shepherd of Hermas and Polycarp, followed by Tertullian and Clement of Alexandria, John Chrysostom and Gregory of Nyssa. According to Karl Heinz Neufeld, S.J., "one is hard pressed not to conclude that Rahner gained during this year an overview of the most important Christian sources of the second century."[26]

Rahner's interests at this time included in addition to the church fathers of East and West, a clear focus on spirituality and mysticism, represented by readings on Ignatian spiritual direction, along with the writings of John Ruysbroeck, Henry Suso, John of the Cross, Blaise Pascal, John Henry Newman, and Francis de Sales. During this period of his life, Rahner also began collaborating with his brother, Hugo Rahner, S.J., professor of church history and patristics and later dean of the theological faculty and president of the University of Innsbruck (1949–1950), on a collection of prayers as well as on work pertaining to patristic studies and to the spirituality of Ignatius of Loyola. The influence of the older brother and highly regarded patristics scholar is acknowledged in Rahner's statement in the foreword to *Aszese und Mystik:* "I have to thank also my brother Hugo for the immense help received."[27]

For more than twenty years, Rahner immersed himself in the great masters and mystics of the church's tradition. His intense studies are well documented by several hundred book re-

views, essays, and lectures produced during that timeframe, beginning with his first publications in the early 1930s. Much of
this foundational work remained invisible to the larger public.
Accumulated diligently into the sum total of a vast reservoir, the
knowledge was never displayed by Rahner for show or bedazzle-
ment. However, it remained accessible to him and if needed
could be instantaneously recalled. In the words of Karl Cardinal
Lehmann, this knowledge was "deposited as if on the quieter
bottom of the sea and [was] waiting there, but immediately [was]
ready when awakened by certain questions, when called upon
and called on to prove itself. Then they all [appeared]: Irenaeus,
Origen, the Cappadocians, Augustine, Thomas of Aquinas,
Bonaventure, Suárez, and last but not least the great mystics."[28]

Theologian and former Jesuit Hans Urs von Balthasar re-
marked on Rahner's uncanny ability to recall the historical
sources of church tradition and doctrine, describing him as
"someone who knows much in the areas of history and theology, but to whom knowledge is only a divining rod that helps
one to identify the underground sources. Often, it is a long,
slow, circling walk, seemingly unfruitful; but suddenly, the rod
jerks and it always jerks accurately. Rahner talks only when he
has discovered something."[29] It is possible that the great reservoir of knowledge that Rahner had built up regarding the early
church, the church fathers, and mystical theology went largely
unrecognized as being formative to Rahner's theology because
he used it merely for the sake of pointing beyond it in framing
and tackling a contemporary theological issue or in answering
a question that believers or non-believers were asking. Perhaps
one could say the same about his familiarity with the two theologians so critical to Rahner's thought, piety, and personal
faith, namely Ignatius of Loyola and Thomas Aquinas.

Ignatius of Loyola

In 1922, three weeks after his final examination in high
school, Rahner entered the novitiate of the Upper German

Province of the Society of Jesus. The house was located in Feldkirch in Vorarlberg, Austria, where he devoted himself to questions of the spiritual life, the life and history of the order, and the study of spiritual classics. Why he wanted to become a Jesuit was not clear to Rahner at the time, though certainly the example of his brother Hugo, who had joined the Jesuits three years earlier, had made an impression on him. His parents heard about Rahner's plans only second-hand, through Rahner's high school teacher. Two years later, in 1924, Rahner published his first article, titled "Why We Need to Pray." The article was undoubtedly influenced by the order's emphasis on prayer and on a personal relationship with God in Christ.

In line with the order's custom, Rahner spent his first year studying philosophy at Feldkirch, then spent two more years studying philosophy at Pullach, near Munich. Based on the copious notebooks in which he summarized his readings, Rahner was deeply impressed with the French writings of the Belgian Jesuit Joseph Maréchal (1878–1944), who had interpreted Thomism in new ways and was concerned also with questions of mysticism and mystical experience. His theme on how the modern person could be understood before God, so relevant to the Jesuit way of life, struck a deep cord with Rahner, so much so that he would later find in Maréchal's interpretation of Thomas Aquinas the inspiration for his 1936 dissertation in philosophy on Thomistic epistemology at the University of Freiburg.

After completing his philosophical studies, Rahner went to study theology at the Jesuit order's school in Valkenburg, the Netherlands. The renewal movement among the Jesuits of the first half of the century was characterized by a revived interest in Ignatius and the *Exercises*. One expression of this interest was Karl and Hugo Rahner's collaboration on an effort to reaffirm the spiritual foundation of the Jesuits by elucidating a theology of prayer in the *Exercises*. According to Herbert Vorgrimler, one of Rahner's first doctoral students, an editorial collaborator, and a keen interpreter of Rahner's theology, "It was out of this concern [for prayer] that Karl Rahner's first major publications emerged in 1932 and 1933: about the doctrine of the spiritual senses in Origen and Bonaventure and the spiritual teaching of Evagrius Ponticus."[30]

The same can be said about Rahner's dissertation in philosophy, which though rejected by the doctoral supervisor, Martin Honecker, was published in 1939 as *Geist in Welt: Zur Metaphysik der endlichen Erkenntnis bei Thomas von Aquin* and translated into many languages, including into English as *Spirit in the World*. As Karl Heinz Neufeld, S.J., has pointed out, Rahner's thoughts in *Spirit in the World* are mostly grounded in "concern with the practice of prayer among the Jesuits, just as conversely the significance of the senses for knowledge in Thomas Aquinas is part of the idea that the human senses have their irreplaceable value in [one's conversation] with God."[31]

This Ignatian orientation and concern with prayer in Rahner is well demonstrated in the 1937 lecture on Ignatius given in Vienna and included in this volume. It is also apparent in the 1938 collection of prayers, *Worte ins Schweigen* (Words Spoken unto Silence) and published in English as *Encounters with Silence*. The silence is, of course, the Silent One, God. Rahner would later affirm the key role played by Ignatian spirituality as he experienced it in the order: "The spirituality of Ignatius himself which we shared in through the practice of prayer and a religious formation has become more significant for me than all learned philosophy and theology inside and outside the Order."[32]

It is surprising that the source of Ignatian spirituality and Ignatian mysticism from which Rahner drew in his theology was often overlooked, so that the "S.J." after his name came to be viewed as a rather private, hence relatively insignificant matter. This oversight was corrected when, on the occasion of his eightieth birthday in 1984, a few weeks before his death, Rahner gave a speech at the University of Freiburg. Titled "Experiences of a Catholic Theologian," the speech identifies as the third of four points critical to his theological enterprise his life in the Jesuit order. "I, for one, hope that my great father in the order, Ignatius of Loyola, would agree that in my theology there is visible a little of his spirit and his unique spirituality." In fact, Rahner expressed "the rather immodest opinion" in the speech "that on this or that point I am nearer to Ignatius than the great Jesuit theology of the Baroque era, which did not always—and certainly not in the significant points—do sufficient justice to a legitimate existentialism in Ignatius (if one may be permitted to call it that)."[33]

Since then, a handful of academic studies—all formerly dissertations—have been published demonstrating that Rahner's theology cannot be properly understood or interpreted without taking into account his background as a Jesuit and his Ignatian spirituality. Among these works should be mentioned the study done by Arno Zahlauer on Rahner's "productive role model" Ignatius of Loyola;[34] the study done by Philip Endean, S.J., on the significance of Ignatian spirituality to Rahner's thought;[35] and the study done by Andreas R. Batlogg, S.J., on Rahner's interpretation and use of "The Mysteries of the Life of Jesus" (which are part of Ignatius's *Exercises*) in his attempt to make accessible the Christian faith.[36]

Rahner was not a Jesuit in name only. He entered the Jesuit novitiate in 1922, professed final vows in 1939, and remained a Jesuit until his death in 1984. His body is buried in the crypt of the Jesuit church at the University of Innsbruck together with many of his Jesuit brothers. During his lifetime, Rahner made the Ignatian exercises regularly, twice the entire thirty-day retreat. And he himself gave them. Between 1934 and 1984, Rahner offered the exercises more than fifty times to retreatants, Jesuits as well as seminarians. But it is likely that he would have offered them to a larger audience, given different circumstances and times. In fact, Ignatius himself had written the *Exercises* as a retreat manual for retreat leaders, so that the exercises could be given to anyone wishing to draw closer to God. He himself gave them to virtually anyone who would ask. And when members of the Society of Jesus, founded in 1540, began serving as confessors and tutors to the nobility and had founded missions and schools, their charges were invited to make the exercises, either individually or in a group.

The purpose of making the exercises is to discern the will of God for one's life, to make an "election," as Ignatius calls it, to say "yes" to God in one's particular place and time in complete human freedom before God. Divided into four "weeks," or stages, the retreat allows participants to see themselves in the light of God, to take account of their sins and the barriers that prevent them from experiencing God's presence with an opportunity for going to confession after the first "week," and to find themselves before the triune God in surrender and readiness to discern, hear, and perceive the divine self-communication meant for them. A fair share of the retreat time is spent in active imagination, in prayer and "colloquies," and in an immersion into the divine mysteries of Jesus' life, passion, death, and resurrection. In that sense, Ignatius's *Exercises* are an invitation to and a preparation for a concrete encounter with Jesus Christ and the Trinitarian God. It is quite possible that Rahner considered Ignatius the first Christian existentialist, someone who not only received the graces of the mystic, replete with visions and ecstatic encounters (of which one finds frequent mention in Ignatius's diaries) but also taught others how to enter into the mystical experience, how to come before the silent God in personal freedom and be open to an authentic, "existential" meeting with God in the person of the loving, suffering Christ.

In 1978, Rahner was asked by the publisher Herder to write a piece for a pictorial monograph on Ignatius of Loyola. He agreed to do this only because both leading experts on Ignatius, one of them his brother Hugo, had died years earlier. Instead of producing a descriptive synopsis of a historical figure, Rahner chose to slip into the role of Ignatius, assuming his persona and translating Ignatian terminology and ideals into modern speech and context. In essence, Rahner did what he had advised earlier, identifying the key elements and teachings of a great mystic so they could assist modern-day seekers. Titled "Speech of Ignatius of Loyola to Today's Jesuit,"[37] the piece is a spiritual tribute to the founder of the order and a reminder to modern-day Jesuits of their spiritual heritage. The speech brings into focus the Jesuit calling and responsibility with regard to the task of guiding souls. In addition, it is a contemporary theological testimony to the classic principles of Ignatian mysticism, a distillation of what mysticism aims for and where it invariably begins, namely in the personal, unmediated encounter with the mysterious, silent God who chooses to reveal himself to the person. Less than thirty pages long in the German edition, the speech is divided into fifteen sections. The first half of the speech addresses the origins and the nature of Ignatian mysticism, while the second offers encouragement and fresh perspectives to the order's members in their mission. To the general reader, the first four sections are of particular interest: they deal with Ignatius's "immediate experience of God," his desire to give "instruction" to others for gaining such an experience, a summary of his "spirituality," and the ways in which the personal God experience relates to the church as an institution.

Rahner says that central to Ignatius's mission and mysticism is his personal experience of God. "You know, I wanted, as I said back then, to 'help souls,' that is, to say something to people about God and his grace and about Jesus Christ, the crucified and risen one, so that their personal freedom would become salvific in the freedom of God. I wanted to say it in a way that it has always been said in the church and still I felt (and this assumption was true) that I was able to say the old in a new way" (p. 10).

What Ignatius wanted to say had come from personal experience, and so he insists, again and again: "I have experienced God, the nameless and unfathomable, the silent and yet near one in the trinity of his attention given to me. I have experienced God also and mainly beyond all visual images; the

one, who when approaching of his own accord and out of
grace, cannot be confused with anything else" (pp. 10–11). It
is surprising that no one seemed "frightened" by the assertion
that "my mysticism gave me such a certainty of faith that it
would remain unshaken even if there did not exist Holy Scripture." For "I have truly met God, the true and living one, the
one who deserves this name that extinguishes all other names.
Whether one calls such an experience 'mysticism' or something else is irrelevant here; how to make clear at all in human
terminology something like that is for your theologians to figure out" (p. 11).

Since Ignatius, according to Rahner, did not presume that
such experienced grace was "a unique privilege of an especially
chosen person," he gave "the exercises to whoever welcomed
such an offer of spiritual help" in the conviction that "God and
the person can encounter one another in a truly immediate
way" (p. 12). It appears that this is "the core of what you commonly call my spirituality." Does it "mark the beginning of the
modern era of the church or does it have perhaps much more
in common with Luther's and Descartes's original experiences
than you Jesuits have been willing to admit through the centuries?" Since people can truly experience God in their heart,
"your pastoral care should always and at every step keep
clearly in mind this goal" (p. 13). At the same time, the church
has "apparently constructed immense and complicated irrigation systems in order to water and make fertile the landscape
of this heart by means of the word, her sacraments, her insti-
tutions, and practices." However besides these waters "piped
in from the outside" (p. 14), there exists, "so to speak, a drilling
station on the landscape itself, so that from such a source, once
tapped, there spring from the land itself the waters of the living spirit unto eternal life, as spoken of by John."

That is not to say that there "exists an ultimate opposition
between this innate source and the 'irrigation system' installed
from the outside." What is meant here is that "such external
pipes of grace are only useful when they meet with this ultimate

grace from within." It is precisely this experience of grace that "I wanted to convey to others through the exercises," which should make it clear now why for Jesuits "the main task around which everything else revolves should be the giving of the exercises"; they are "a mystagogical help for others so that they will not be pushing aside the immediacy of God but will clearly experience and accept it" (p. 15).

The central task of Jesuits, then, both now and in the future is to offer people "help for the immediate experience of God where they realize that the incomprehensible mystery that we call God is near, can be addressed, and shelters us in a salvific way, especially when we do not want to domesticate it but surrender ourselves to it unconditionally" (pp. 15–16).

In 1983, a year before his death, Rahner called the essay on Ignatius "a sort of last will and testament." He had reached this conclusion some years after having written the piece and upon re-reading it. To Rahner, it contains the key themes of his theological enterprise and is "a résumé of my theology, in general, and of how I tried to live."[38]

Thomas Aquinas

Early on in his theological studies, Rahner had been selected by his superiors to teach the history of philosophy at the Jesuit school in Pullach, near Munich. He was sent to his hometown, Freiburg, to study for the doctorate in philosophy between 1934 and 1936. There he had the good fortune of having Martin Heidegger as one of his teachers. However, due to Heidegger's Nazi leanings, Rahner selected Martin Honecker as his dissertation director. As mentioned earlier, Honecker eventually rejected the dissertation, a creative interpretation of Thomas Aquinas's epistemology. In the meantime, Rahner had been reassigned by his order to teach theology in Innsbruck, so the failure meant little to him. In 1936, the same year in which he had submitted his dissertation for review at Freiburg, Rahner had also submitted a dissertation in theology at Innsbruck where he completed his doctoral studies. In the spring of 1937, he received word that Honecker had rejected the Aquinas dissertation because it lacked the character of historical Thomas interpretations. It was indeed true that Rahner was not interested in Thomistic thought per se but rather in "the weight and dynamics of Thomas's basic thoughts, which he objectively developed in a fresh and carefree manner."[39] Based on Rahner's previous publications, he was granted the teaching privilege at a university and was appointed professor of theology at Innsbruck, where he began lecturing in the winter semester of 1937. Only a year later the Nazis took over and closed the theological faculty; the following year they closed the Jesuit seminary.

The influence of Heidegger on Rahner's thought has often been exaggerated. Rahner himself tried to fend off such speculation. "Some people who talk about my theology often exaggerate the influence of Heidegger. It is an exaggeration that takes no notice of the simple fact that Heidegger did not teach theology and I am explicitly a theologian and not a 'philosopher,'" he says. Instead, Heidegger's "influence relates to a certain way of thinking. It was less a matter of content than [the method of] questioning certain assumptions."[40] The interpretations of Rahner's work during the 1960s and 1970s had been fixated on the transcendental philosophical and transcendental theological aspects, blending out the spiritual and mystical.

According to Andreas R. Batlogg, S.J., "the ordinary, daily responsibilities that Father Rahner met faithfully for decades in his roles of priest and Jesuit shaped him also in his theology, at least much more so than some would want or are able to acknowledge." This means that the Ignatian influence in his thought "makes up perhaps for a third, the other third is certainly neo-scholasticism, which to my generation is completely unknown, and another third is certainly a type of individual creation, aided by the type of thinking that he had learned from Martin Heidegger." [41]

It is precisely today's "unknown" neo-scholasticism, derived from Thomas Aquinas and taught in Latin at the time, that permeated theological education and interpretation. Scholasticism had begun in the Baroque era as Thomism and continued up to Rahner's own time in the form of neo-scholasticism. Rahner gives an extensive account of his relationship to Thomas Aquinas and Thomas's influence on him in a 1982 interview, published in *Faith in a Wintry Season*.[42] Though theological education was supposedly grounded in the thought of Thomas, Rahner says that students' "contact with Thomas must really be described as extraordinarily slight" (p. 42).

For example, the textbook *De gratia* ("On Grace") of his teacher Hermann Lange, S.J., "discussed Thomas in a very precise historical fashion," but it was more as "a sort of reverence, a mere decoration," which meant "I certainly didn't have a living and inspirational contact with Thomas then" (p. 42). Only the reading of Joseph Maréchal, S.J., allowed Rahner to meet Thomas "in a more personal way," producing what would be later called Rahner's "transcendental philosophy and theology."

Rahner contrasts his own understanding of Thomas, and that of his generation of Jesuits, with that of the Dominicans. Since Thomas was a Dominican, the Dominicans revered him as their great father in the faith. By contrast, the Jesuits read him as a great father of the church, so that "we allowed him to alert us to certain problems, but ultimately we approached him with our own questions and statement of problems. And so we didn't really practice a Thomistic scholasticism, but tried to maintain toward him a stance comparable to that toward Augustine, Origen, and other great thinkers." In short, Thomas was "for us by no means a boring and dry scholastic, but someone with whom we wanted a real encounter..." (p. 45).

Rahner has often been called a theologian of a particular issue, a "*Gelegenheitstheologe*" or "*Anlaßtheologe*," someone who could and would speak to any contemporary topic and bring into focus its bearings upon the human condition and the church in relation to a transcendent God. Nothing seemed too complicated or farfetched for him to address. Quite possibly, Rahner had mustered the courage to tackle even the most complex or seemingly off-limits theological questions facing people and the church because he had observed this courage in Thomas, had observed how the so-called Angelic Doctor and patron saint of theological studies had approached the questions of his own time by means of a construct of careful reasoning and argument. Moreover, Rahner learned from Thomas that no "scientific," intellectually solid theology can be done without philosophy. A theology that sacrifices the mind and starts "from a positivism in faith" will "ultimately lack self-understanding." Therefore, theology needs philosophy, "and it makes no difference which philosophy one is dealing with. What is important is that philosophy give an account of its own reflection and be brought into theology after it has been subjected to such philosophical reflection. We have to learn at least this from Thomas" (pp. 46–47). The lack of philosophical reflection in theology may have induced modern theology to turn too quickly to the world, imagining God in the world's terms and co-opting God to meet the world's desires and needs. In Rahner's view, "modern theology's turn to the world too often fails to see that it all too quickly takes God as a stopgap for human beings, their happiness and their so-called self-realization." To him, "That is the greatest profanity and shamelessness toward God!" For "God is not there for us," rather "we are there for him" and "we are real Christians only when we let ourselves fall, in surrender and without condition, into the incomprehensibility of God along with Jesus the Crucified" (pp. 50–51).

So what are the mystical aspects of Thomas that influenced Rahner's thought and his own mysticism? In addition to what Rahner says about Thomas as mystic in the essay included in this volume, three further observations can be made. First, Rahner stresses "Thomas's basic conviction that to be and to be present to oneself are the same or that freedom is merely the self-actualization of the person" (pp. 52–53). By responding positively to God's self-communication, by saying "yes" to God, we become utterly free, we become completely ourselves, even though at first sight our freedom appears to be curbed. Second, Rahner is drawn to both the spiritual devotion and the sobriety of Thomas that keep each other in check. With "all the spiritual devotion that can be found in him, he is more sober and realistic than many another medieval theologian," so that "his spirituality emerges as more restrained than that of many another medieval theologian, including Bonaventure." And third, Rahner stresses the incomprehensibility of God, a point found in Thomas also, even though "I don't think he brought it sufficiently to bear upon the basic framework of his theology" (p. 53). Rahner has developed this aspect of Thomas's thought extensively in his own writings and it can be found in nearly each piece—whether prayer, sermon, or essay—contained in this volume.

Reading one of the greatest theologians of our time through the lens of a mystic is no small task. The main burden falls on the reader. In commenting on criticisms leveled against Rahner's work, Philip Endean, S.J., correctly says that "the problem is not that Rahner's theology and spiritual vision have been tried and found wanting: they have been found difficult and left untried."[43] Framing Rahner's writings from the mystical perspective is intended to facilitate a reading that may, in fact, seem difficult at first because untried. The hope is that ultimately readers will find in Rahner a modern-day master teacher and mystic, someone who by his piety and sobriety can give us the courage to pray, see, and live as mystics in everyday life, thus allowing for our concrete encounter with the mysterious, incomprehensible triune God.

Notes

1. Karl Rahner, *Worte ins Schweigen* (Innsbruck: Felizian Rauch Verlag, 1938); or *Encounters with Silence*, trans. James M. Demske (Westminster, MD: The Newman Press, 1960).

2. Karl Rahner, *Von der Not und dem Segen des Gebetes* (Innsbruck: Felizian Rauch Verlag, 1949); translated into English as *On*

Prayer (New York: Paulist Press, 1968); then as *The Need and the Blessing of Prayer: A New Translation of Father Rahner's Book on Prayer*, trans. Bruce W. Gillette, introduction by Harvey D. Egan, S.J. (Collegeville, MN: The Liturgical Press, 1997).

3. The background information was graciously supplied by Andreas R. Batlogg, S.J., director of the Rahner Archives in Munich, co-editor of Karl Rahner's *Sämtliche Werke*, and resident Jesuit minister at St. Michael's Church, Munich.

4. See Nikolaus Schwerdtfeger, *Gnade und Welt* (Freiburg: Herder, 1983), 164–211; summarized in Herbert Vorgrimler, *Karl Rahner: Gotteserfahrung in Leben und Denken* (Darmstadt: Wissenschaftliche Buchgesellschaft, 2004), 178.

5. Karl Rahner, *Glaube, der die Erde liebt* (Freiburg: Herder, 1966); in English, *Everyday Faith*, trans. W. J. O'Hara (New York: Herder and Herder, 1968).

6. Karl Rahner, "Teresa of Avila: Doctor of the Church," in Karl Rahner, *Opportunities for Faith: Elements of a Modern Spirituality*, trans. Edward Quinn (New York: Seabury Press, 1974), 125.

7. Ibid.

8. Ibid., 123.

9. Ibid., 126.

10. Karl Rahner, "Christian Living Formerly and Today," in Karl Rahner, *Theological Investigations*, vol. 7, trans. David Burke (New York: Herder and Herder, 1971), 15.

11. Karl Rahner, *Meditations on the Sacraments*, trans. Salvator Attanasio, James M. Quigley, S.J., and Dorothy White (New York: Seabury Press, 1977), xi; published originally as *Die Siebenfältige Gabe* (Munich: Verlag Ars Sacra Joseph Mueller, 1974).

12. Ibid.

13. Ibid., xvi.

14. Ibid., xvii.

15. Karl Rahner, *Faith in a Wintry Season: Interviews and Conversations with Karl Rahner in the Last Years of His Life, 1982–84*, ed. Hubert Biallowons, Harvey D. Egan, S.J., and Paul Imhof, S.J. (New York: Crossroad, 1990), 115.

16. Harvey D. Egan, S.J., *Karl Rahner: Mystic of Everyday Life* (New York: Crossroad, 1998), 55.

17. Ibid., 57.

18. Karl Rahner, "Religious Enthusiasm and the Experience of Grace," in Karl Rahner, *Theological Investigations*, vol. 16, trans. David Morland (London: Darton, Longman and Todd), 35–51; in Egan, *Karl Rahner*, 70.

19. Rahner, *Faith in a Wintry Season*, p. 35.

20. Ibid.

21. *Karl Rahner in Dialogue: Conversations and Interviews, 1965–1982*, ed. Hubert Biallowons, Harvey D. Egan, S.J., and Paul Imhof, S.J. (New York: Crossroad, 1986), 297.

22. Rahner, *Faith in a Wintry Season*, 16.

23. Hans Urs von Balthasar, S.J., *Stimmen der Zeit* 136 (1939): 334.

24. Karl Heinz Neufeld, S.J., *Die Brüder Rahner: Eine Biographie* (Freiburg: Herder, 1994/2004), 135.

25. Karl Rahner, "E Latere Christi: Der Ursprung der Kirche als zweiter Eva aus der Seite Christi des zweiten Adam. Eine Untersuchung über den typologischen Sinn von Joh 19, 34," ed. Andreas R. Batlogg, S.J., in Karl Rahner, *Sämtliche Werke*, vol. 3 (Freiburg: Herder, 1999), 3–84, 428–35, 449.

26. Neufeld, *Die Brüder Rahner*, 99.

27. Marcel Viller, S.J., and Karl Rahner, S.J., *Aszese und Mystik in der Väterzeit* (Freiburg: Herder, 1939), preface.

28. Karl Cardinal Lehmann, "Karl Rahners Bedeutung für die Kirche" in *Stimmen der Zeit*, "Karl Rahner—100 Jahre," Spezial 1 (2004): 11.

29. Hans Urs von Balthasar, "Größe und Last der Theologie heute. Einige grundsäzliche Gedanken zu zwei Aufsatzbänden Karl Rahners," in *Wort und Wahrheit* 10 (1955): 533.

30. Herbert Vorgrimler, *Understanding Karl Rahner: An Introduction to His Life and Thought* (New York: Crossroad, 1986), 57.

31. See ibid.

32. *Karl Rahner im Gespräch*, ed. Paul Imhof, S.J., and Hubert Biallowons, vol. 2 (Munich: Kösel Verlag, 1983), 51; Vorgrimler, *Understanding Karl Rahner*, 57.

33. Karl Rahner, *Von der Unbegreiflichkeit Gottes: Erfahrungen eines katholischen Theologen*, ed. Albert Raffelt (Freiburg: Herder, 2004), 46.

34. Arno Zahlauer, *Karl Rahner und sein "produktives Vorbild" Ignatius von Loyola* (Innsbruck: Tyrolia, 1996).

35. Philip Endean, S.J., *Karl Rahner and Ignatian Spirituality* (New York: Oxford University Press, 2001); see also Philip Endean, S.J., "Introduction" to *Karl Rahner: Spiritual Writings*, ed. Philip Endean, S.J. (Maryknoll, NY: Orbis Books, 2004), 9–30.

36. Andreas Batlogg, S.J., *Die Mysterien des Leben Jesu bei Karl Rahner. Zugang zum Christusglauben* (Innsbruck: Tyrolia, 2001).

37. Karl Rahner, "Rede des Ignatius von Loyola an einen Jesuiten heute," in *Ignatius von Loyola* (Freiburg: Herder, 1978), 9–38; translated as "Ignatius of Loyola Speaks to a Modern Jesuit," in Karl Rahner, *Ignatius of Loyola*, with a historical introduction by Paul Imhof, S.J., color photographs by Helmut Nils Loose, and trans. Rosaleen Ockenden (Cleveland: Collins, 1979); the references (hereinafter cited in the text) are to the German edition.

38. Rahner, *Faith in a Wintry Season*, 104.

39. Lehmann, "Karl Rahners Bedeutung für die Kirche," 5.

40. *Glaube in winterlicher Zeit*, 13; quoted in Neufeld, *Die Brüder Rahner*, 110–11.

41. Andreas R. Batlogg, S.J., "Interpret des Ignatius von Loyola," in *Begegnungen mit Karl Rahner: Weggefährten erinnern sich*, ed. Andreas R. Batlogg, S.J., and Melvin E. Michalski (Freiburg: Herder, 2006), 278–79.

42. "The Importance of Thomas Aquinas: Interview with Jan van den Eijnden, Innsbruck (May 1982)" in *Faith in a Wintry Season*, 41–58 (references hereinafter cited in the text).

43. Endean, "Introduction" to *Karl Rahner: Spiritual Writings*, 29.

ADVENT

THE JUDGMENT OF THE SON OF MAN
Luke 21:25-33

It is a strange thing. At the beginning of our preparation for Christmas, the gospel is about the end of the world. And yet, it is not surprising. For what is already contained in a small beginning is most easily recognized in its great ending. What is truly meant by the arrival of the Savior with his great "advent," what has already happened there, is best seen in the completion of this arrival, which we commonly and somewhat mistakenly call his "second advent." In reality, it is the completion of his *one* advent that is still in progress.

This is why our church's Advent is not a mere remembering of something that has gone by, but people's entry in faith and hope and love into a development that started when God himself stepped into the history of his world and made this history his own, so that it would proceed inevitably toward the day that today's gospel reading puts prophetically before us. It is a picture of completion, intended to help us see what in truth is already happening in the depth of our life and our existence, though it happens inconspicuously and quietly, and hence is easily overlooked by our sinful blindness. God is already under way, is secretly already here, and the revelation of his presence is in progress.

But if it is to be apparent that God is already here, then we will see him as the Son of Man, as one of our own. We will see him as one who has lived his life among ours, a life that is the way ours is: short, bitter, and dark. As the Son of Man, God will then ask us about our life. At this tribunal, we will not be able to say that he, the eternal one living in the harmony of his eternity, could not really imagine what our life is like with its weak moments and unsolved riddles. He not only has imagined it but has also literally lived it. He himself has become human. Not the distant God, but the Son of Man will be the judgment and the justification of our life. The person who is God will be our judgment. Because he is human, he knows well the human condition, but he also takes to heart as the eternally distant God our reality. On the basis of personal experience he takes it to heart in the way only a human being could love what is human and hate what is inhumane in humans.

Is it more blessed or more dangerous to be judged by a human being and not solely by a God who was not personally present in the story that is being judged? Who can say? The gospel does. The Son of Man is in charge of the judgment. But if our judgment is carried out by the human being who is God, and if by his arrival he is already walking our path with us from the cradle to the grave, then the face of the Son of Man, from whom we will be able to read our verdict, is already looking at us mysteriously through every human face we see, since all are his brothers and sisters. This face is looking at us through the pure face of the child, the worn face of the poor, the tear-stained face of the sinner, even the bitter face of our so-called opponent and enemy. One day, we will "lift our heads" and will have to look into the face of the one who is coming as the Son of Man, since he is the God of eternity. And from his face everyone will be looking at us: all those around us because of whom we are guilty and those too by whom we did right. One voice will come out of his mouth: What you have done to the least of these my brothers and sisters . . . or left undone. The voice we hear from him will never grow silent and will fill eternity from one end to the other. Will we be able to raise our heads to the face of the Son of Man with the confidence of the redeemed and the living?

FESTIVAL OF FAITH
Matthew 11:2–10

The Baptist stands in the middle of the Advent season. Here, into *our* Advent, he fits well. For is not our life still Advent: faith, expectation, patience, and longing for what cannot yet be grasped? Are we not expected, as Christians, to build houses upon what is "only" hoped for and believed? If we want to be Christians, are we not often compelled to act like the fools of God and release the sparrow from our hand while the dove is still sitting on heaven's roof—the sparrow of financial advantage, of physical enjoyment, of forceful insistence on being right—for the sake of the heavenly kingdom, a kingdom that, alas, no one has seen yet?

Into this Advent of expectation of what is yet to come, the Baptist of today's gospel fits well. He is what we are supposed to be in our lifelong Advent. He is in prison. He was careless enough to tell the head of state what he really thought. How could one have demonstrated such a lack of political savvy! He is locked up. That serves him right. And no one will get him out. Friends do not stage a revolt. They have too little clout for that anyhow, are interested only in theology, and are fairly inept in what really matters in life (or so it seems). And even God leaves his preacher of repentance locked up. God seems to be occupied with weightier matters. God works miracles through his son, even if these miracles cure only a few poor souls who seem to be rather irrelevant as far as the king-dom of God goes. One does not know whether to laugh or to cry about it. These miracles do nothing to help the holy prophet, the blood relative and official forerunner of the one doing them. The prophet remains locked up until the bitter end.

It is not easy to sit in prison as the prophet who is finished prophesying, waiting for certain death and taking an interest in miracles that are of no help whatsoever to one's own situation. But the Baptist is no reed that is moved by the wind of the world. He has faith in spite of it all. He is the messenger preparing the way for God first and foremost in his own life and heart, preparing the way for the God who is taking such a terribly long time to arrive and does not even hurry up a little when a prophet of his is at the point of being killed, the God who seems to be arriving only when it is already too late. The Baptist knows that God will be proved right in the end, that God will win by losing, that God is alive and gives life by being killed himself, that God is the future that appears to have none. In a word, the Baptist believes. It is difficult for him. His heart is bitter and his sky is dark. His heart's question sounds a bit forced: Are you the one supposed to come? But this question is asked of the right person, of God become human. One is permitted in a prayerful attitude to show God one's trembling heart, a heart that is almost at wits' end and is running out of strength. In a prayerful heart, there always remains faith enough to receive an answer that suffices: Go and tell John what you have seen... and blessed are those not turned off by me, even if they are deserted and in prison.

All our life we are in Advent, since we Christians are still waiting for the one yet to come. Then only will it be said that we were right. Before then, however, the world seems to be right. The world will laugh while you are crying, the Lord says. We, too, are sitting in prison: in the prison of death, of unanswered questions, of our own weakness, of our own pitiful state, of misery and the tragedy of life. We will not get out alive. But daily we will want to send off messengers of our faith and of our prayer to the one who is yet to come to judge the living and the dead. These Advent-like messengers will always come back to us to report: See, I am coming; blessed are those not turned off by me.

PATIENCE WITH THE PRELIMINARY

Again the Baptist has come into our Advent and our Advent expectation. And one asks him: What are you doing here, since you are not the true, long-expected Messiah? This kind of question is only too familiar to us. People can display the most disconcerting and dangerous impatience when it comes to Advent, waiting for God, the burning longing for the eternal. They demonstrate a religious radicalism that looks fabulous and grandiose but is, in reality, the opposite of the attitude of those who are true Advent people.

People are thirsting for God, yearning for him, hoping that he will soon establish his kingdom. They want the absolute, the blinding truth that completely burns away any doubt. They want the radical goodness that will destroy any fear, so that goodness ends up looking like another form of selfishness. Instead, it is only the messengers that are coming; everything is tentative; mere people in their humanity and in their inhumanity are the messengers of God; mere human ceremonies (called sacraments) appear as God's salvific acts. And all these preliminaries are saying the same: I am not the real and not the true thing; the true and the real are still hidden in all the ordinariness of words, of people, of signs.

Is it any wonder that people—who remain sinners even when they are very religious—are losing patience? They are saying: Why do human beings, words, and signs have to show up in religion when they are not the real thing, when they are not the unveiled God of naked immediacy? Those who are particularly impatient even assume that one can find God apart from people, from words, and from the signs of the church, in such things as nature, or the infinite depths of their hearts, or the type of political activism that wants to establish right now and forever, by force, the kingdom of God without God, or in other things. But finally they realize—

quite frequently too late—that they have ended up in the desert of their own empty hearts where the demons live, not God; in the loveless wilderness of blind and brutal nature, which is benevolent only on Sunday afternoons; in the sparse wilderness of the world, where the waters of one's ideals dissipate the more deeply one walks into them; in the hopeless arena of politics, which manages to bring about only the mere tyranny of force instead of the reign of God.

No, there is no way around it. We will have to listen to the voice of the one calling in the wilderness, even though he says: I am not the one. We will have to muster the patience of the true Advent person. The church is only the voice of one calling in the wilderness, a voice saying that the ultimate, the glorious kingdom of God, is yet to come, but only when he wills it and not when we would like it. We cannot disregard this voice simply because it comes out of the mouths of people; we cannot ignore the messenger of the church simply because he is not worthy to untie the shoestrings of his master, the one he is announcing, or because he is not able to call down fire from heaven the way Elijah did. It is simply still Advent. Even the church is still an Advent church, for we are still waiting for the one to come in revealed splendor of absolute divinity along with the eternal kingdom.

And this church is always saying the right thing to those who are impatient and want to see God right away: Why don't you prepare the true way for this God, the way of faith, of love, of humility, the way of patience that is lined with all its small, preliminary messengers and with their poor words and small signs? Then surely God will come. For God comes only to those who patiently show love for God's forerunners and the preliminary. The Pharisees in the gospel, however, those who rejected the forerunner of the Messiah since he was not the real and the true one, also missed the true one when he came.

THE TROUBLE WITH SALVATION HISTORY
Luke 3:1–6

It will be the ongoing problem of Christianity, of Christ himself and of his church, that they are "historical." Precisely in the fifteenth year of Emperor Tiberius, it says, precisely in Judea and Galilee, precisely under these specific rulers of old, Pilate and his Annas and Caiaphas. Why could humanity's salvation not start where everything else does? Why not everywhere and always? Is the distance to the God of eternity, to whom the whole world belongs, not the same from any place and at all times?

But no, back then and there, the word of the Lord came to John and this started the decisive era of salvation. And it has remained that way. We have to be baptized with water, of all things, and one cannot do without. We have to acquiesce to hearing the word of forgiveness for our sins spoken to us concretely on a Saturday afternoon in a wooden box, called a confessional, by a human voice and not merely by the quiet voice of God heard in the depths of our heart. And yet, the beautiful presence of God is not the church itself with the body of the one who back then under Pontius Pilate suffered for us on the cross. The words in the catechism, not the ideas in the realm of metaphysics, are the truths by which we can live and die.

God can find people wherever they are stuck by no fault of their own and where they have a clean conscience. And, in his boundless mercy, God will do so without us having to see to it. But this does not mean that we may dictate to him where it is that we would like to be found by him. God can walk all paths. But we, as his creatures, may walk only the paths prescribed for us by him.

God has prescribed for us a distinct path of salvation. It is not true that all our paths lead to God. God has intimated certain ones to us, so that we may recognize and acknowledge that salvation is *his* grace, his free and unconditional gift, and not an entitlement owed to us by God. We need to recognize and acknowledge that God is not at our disposal but that we are to be at his, that God is God and we are his creatures. God has outlined for us certain paths of salvation because he himself, out of unsurpassed mercy, wished to walk them, because he himself wished to be a human being the way we are, imprisoned by space and time and history from which no one in this world can ever truly escape. He himself was born under the reign of Emperor Augustus, in Nazareth of all places (from which no good ever comes), suffered under Pontius Pilate, was imprisoned at precisely the then-and-there of date and location of a true human being. What sweet grace of a humane God! We need not look for God in his eternal kingdom, where we would only end up hopelessly lost as in an emptiness devoid of any paths.

Truly, Christianity is so human, so historical, that it is too human for many people who think a true religion ought to be non-human, that is to say, independent of the senses and a-historical. Instead, the word became flesh. In the fifteenth year of Emperor Tiberius, the word of the Lord went out to John. And this is how it has remained. Christianity is a historical and a rather concrete and earthy religion. It is a problem for the proud, those who at least as far as religion goes do not want to be human, but it is the grace and the truth of those who humbly desire to be human in space and time, even though they are praying to the God of eternity and infinitude.

CHRISTMAS

THE REPLY OF SILENCE
Letter to a Friend

Christmas? This word is said almost with some degree of reticence, because one wonders if it is really possible to make clear to another what is meant by the term "celebrating Christmas." This feast certainly cannot be explained simply by Christmas trees, gifts, a cozy home, and similarly touching customs observed with mild skepticism for the sake of honoring traditions. So what is there beyond that? Well, I will dare offer you something of a recipe.

The great experiences in life may be a matter of destiny, gifts of God and God's mercy, yet they tend to be mostly given to those who are prepared to receive them. Otherwise, the star may rise over a person's life yet remain unrecognized. For great moments of wisdom, of art, of love, one has to prepare both in body and soul; the same goes for the great festival days of our salvation. Therefore, do not let them simply happen, do not enter them with ill will and in an ordinary fashion. Prepare yourself, be willing to prepare; that's the first thing.

And here is the second thing: Take courage to be alone. Only when you have really managed that, when you have done so from a Christian perspective, can you hope to offer a Christmas-like heart, hence a tender, patient, courageously braced, quietly gentle heart to those to whom you are trying to show love. This offering is the true gift beneath the Christmas tree, for without it all the other gifts are only items of meaningless expense, items that could have been given on any other occasion as well. So, try to stay with yourself for a little while. Perhaps you can find a room where you are able to be alone. Or perhaps you know of a quiet walking path or a silent church.

Don't talk to yourself there as you would with people, as if discussing things with them and arguing, even though they are not present. Wait. Listen. Do not expect the extraordinary to happen. Empty yourself, but not in an accusatory way or by reveling in yourself. Permit yourself to encounter your self. Perhaps this will make you feel rather miserable. You may begin to realize how far away are those with whom you have daily dealings and those with whom you consider yourself bonded in love. Perhaps you will not feel anything but an ominous experience of emptiness and deadness.

Endure it. You will come to realize that everything that is called up in such silence is framed by a nameless distance, as if permeated by something that seems like emptiness. Do not call it God yet! It is only that which points toward God and which allows us by its namelessness and limitlessness to fathom that God is something different from simply one more thing, added to other things we generally deal with. We are allowed to behold God's presence when we are still and do not flee in fright from the ominous—which lives and does its work in silence—not even fleeing to the Christmas tree or to more concretely religious representations, which have the capacity to kill religion.

But this is only the beginning, only the preparation of a Christmas celebration for you. If you are able to remain within yourself and allow the silence to speak of God, then this silence that calls out loudly becomes mysteriously ambiguous. It is both the fear of death and the proclamation of eternity that graciously draws close to you, and both are too close together and too similar for us to be able to discern on our own the distant and yet near eternity. But precisely in this disquietude are we able to understand ourselves and to accept the sweet quieting of disquietude. And that is precisely the Christmas message: God is truly near to you, especially where you are open to this eternal dimension. And then the distance of God becomes also God's inconceivable, all-permeating nearness.

God is gently present. He says: Do not be afraid! He is enclosed in the interior cell. Trust this closeness, for it is not emptiness. Let go, and then you will find. Give up, and then you will be rich. For because of your internal experience you need no longer rely on that which is tangibly concrete, on that which is particular and can be held onto. You have now both the tangible and the eternal that has drawn near. That is how you ought to interpret your interior experience, perceiving it as the great festival of the divine descent of eternity into time, of infinity into temporality, as the wedding of God with his creature. Such a festival happens inside you—theologians refer to it dryly as "grace"—and it happens within you when you remain quiet, when you wait and interpret in faith, hope, and love correctly, meaning from the perspective of Christmas, that which you are experiencing.

Only the experience of the heart allows one to truly grasp the faith message of Christmas: God has become human. We generally say this so casually. We imagine this incarnation as if God were dressing up in costume, so that God remains in essence still God and we cannot be sure whether God is really where we are. When we say that God has become human, we do not mean he has ceased being God in the limitless vastness of his glory. Neither do we mean that the human side in him is something that does not really affect him or is only adopted and does not say anything about him but only says something about us. God has become human, and that really says something about God.

We should not view the humanity of God as this common characteristic that has its counterpart in God's divinity.

Neither should we view it as something that permanently lingers in the background and can be tagged onto God, tied to him verbally with a hollow "and." In seeing the human side of God, we need to interpret it as God himself being present. When we simply place divinity next to humanity in the incarnate Word of the Father instead of understanding that both are one and the same, we run the risk of missing the place where the blessed mystery of Christmas settles into our transcendental existence and enters our life and our history as our salvation.

But do not forget: According to the testimony of faith, Jesus is truly human, which means he is like you and me—a finite, free, human being who obediently accepts the inconceivable mystery of his existence, one who has to respond and does, one who is asked a question and hears it, the question that is eternal and can be answered only in this ultimate act of the heart, which surrenders lovingly and obediently to the eternal mystery in an act in which acceptance happens through the one who himself is accepted. And it is this same one whose beginning you desire to celebrate. Because he accepted as a human being, you, too, can dare to do as he did: to quietly and confidently call the incomprehensible one "Father," to be open to the incomprehensible one not as a deathly distance and a devastating verdict on account of our pitiful condition, but as immeasurable, merciful nearness. All this because he is both God and human being: giver, gift, and acceptance, call and reply at once.

It would be good to appeal to the experience of one's heart so as to perceive inwardly what the incarnation of the eternal God really means. It would be good to allow this to happen in stillness, where one is consciously alone with oneself. This stillness, correctly understood as faith in the message of Christmas, is the experience of human existence as eternal, an experience that occurs only because God himself became human. God would not have been born as a human being had we been meant to experience our existence differently.

When we accept that which is silently incomprehensible, which envelops us as both the faraway and the overwhelmingly near, as the sheltering closeness and the mild love that does not hold back; when we have the courage to understand ourselves in a way made possible only by grace and faith—whether we know it or not—then we have understood in faith what it means to know the grace of Christmas. Though very simple, this is the peace graciously announced to us out of divine favor.

THE GREAT JOY

Christmas Eve

Let us celebrate Christmas, a feast of faith and of love for the Word that became flesh, a feast of love also among us, because people can now love others since God himself became human. Let us adore God, since God loved the human being and the poor human creature so much that he placed it for all eternity amidst the burning flame of his divinity, never to be extinguished. Incomprehensible God, adventurer of love! We had thought that the sorry human creature could only be a primitive, poorly designed prototype for the super human being that is yet to come. It surely is hard to live with ourselves the way we are and even more so in the company of others. People are hard to put up with, and understandably so, since they continually make mistakes and go from one extreme to another.

And still: He remained undeterred by the womb of a virgin —at least that is what the church says of him in its litany. He himself came into his own creation, into the form of a human being. Had this not happened, it is questionable whether we could have had the courage to believe that God's work had succeeded. He himself has crawled into everything that confines people, a confinement made apparent by the infinite distance between him and us: the narrowness of the womb, the narrowness of a run-down homeland with its occupying forces, the narrowness of the hopeless situation of the time, a closed-minded environment, a convoluted political situation, a body destined to die, the prison of not being understood, the monotony of daily life, the experience of complete failure, the dark night of being God-forsaken, and death. He did not skip any of it. But the confining space into which God himself has stepped needs an exit. Since God was not satisfied with himself but wanted to become one of these human beings instead, God's becoming human had to have been clearly worth the effort. When God is among people as their brother, humanity is no longer a herd but a holy family. The tragedy that is human history has to have a blessed ending since God did not just look from the distant throne of his eternity at this non-divine comedy but entered the stage himself in as serious a manner as the rest of us who have no choice.

The so-called true reality of those who are bitter, disappointed, and superficial is being diffused now and taken seriously only by unbelieving fools who are greedily reaching for it, since God himself now stands behind and has become himself the true reality underneath the surface: Eternity is already at the core of time, life is at the core of death, truth is stronger than the lie, love is more powerful than hate, human malice has already been fully conquered by God's grace. Christianity has a positive view of humans and such a view could only have been created by God. It is little wonder that God then seems so unreal to us. There is no need for a super human being when God himself has become a human being. A pure humanism has become outdated when the human being has become God through the son of the Father and the virgin, as the church fathers say, and when the human being is far more than a human being. Therefore, it is appropriate for us to be demanding. In fact, we can never be demanding enough with regard to God; we are not allowed to wish for anything less than being the brother of the eternal Word of the Father, the Word who became flesh.

Let us go and be good, then, at least on this day, in this holy night. Perhaps we will realize that it is not so difficult and that we can let this attitude even carry over into the new year. Let us be good. We are not entitled to demand a better world unless we have begun this betterment in our own hearts. Let us be good today. Do we not see that there is no need of defending ourselves against others by being ambitious and fearful, malicious and bitter? God has come. And God, who is everything, cannot be taken away from us. He is our brother. Hence, it is appropriate to carry love for our neighbor and mercy for others also in our own heart, to have a mild heart, a heart that forgives, a heart that hopes, is quiet and joyous, faithful and without guile. God himself has tried on such a heart and is telling us that it can be done. His experience is more important and reliable than our own; we can be better than we think. More can be made of us than we assume. With Christ formed in us, we can never reach high enough. We are far more than we are able to imagine.

So, let us sing with the joy of a heart that has been freed to live in union with God, who is eternal youth. The night has turned to light and God has prepared a feast for himself that previously did not exist in heaven: God has become human. Heaven and earth are ringing in God's still, holy night, which is brighter than the dreary human day: Glory to God, peace to people in whom God has delighted. Let us bow down and read the gospel with joyous hearts: At that time, a decree went out from Emperor Augustus...

HOLY NIGHT

Why do we call the feast that we celebrate today Holy Night? We do not know for sure from a historical perspective whether Jesus was born at night. The story of the shepherds, tending their flocks by night and then hearing the heavenly news about the birth of the Savior, is in and of itself no clear proof that Jesus was actually born at night. And yet, Christianity has always imagined this blessed and saving birth to have happened at night. The German language has carried this conviction even into the name of this feast day, *"Weihnacht,"* Holy Night. Why?

Night has a dual meaning for people. Like almost everything in human existence, night has metaphorical meaning and hence is ambiguous. Night can be that which is ominous and dark, the time when no one can do any work, as Jesus says in scripture; night is seen as related to death; it is the time of non-existence, of the uncertain and the dangerous, of the unclear. And therefore even in religious thought night can have that same symbolic meaning: in scripture, night is considered the time of unbelief and of sin, the time of judgment and divine summons. It is the reason why Christians are to be children of the day, have to shine like stars in the night so as to not be taken by surprise at the arrival of the judge who comes like a thief in the night. Therefore, we have to stay awake, we must not sleep, we have to get up from sleep and walk as if it were day.

But from the human perspective, also expressed in scripture, night has yet another face. Night is the time of silence and of gathered strength that restrains itself, that can wait and allow things to ripen. In the middle of the night, the call goes out that the bridegroom is coming. Night is in scripture the time of heavenly dreams. Since night is a time of detachment from enslaving ideas and ties to the visible everyday world, it is also a time of prayer, so that Jesus spends entire nights in conversation with God. The night can even be perceived as a tender creature of God, so that the psalmist can pray: Yours is the day and yours is the night (Ps 74:16). And Daniel demands of the night that it praise God (Dan 3:71) since, according to the psalmist, each night passes on to the next the message of God's glory and the heavens already declare God's quiet grandeur and his immeasurable magnitude to those who believe (Ps 19:1–3).

Why is it that we can perceive the night in such opposite ways? We experience the night as the beginning, as the unde-termined, as that which has yet to be made clear and concrete: the light and the day. The beginning, the possibility, is what is ambiguous: the rich promise, which has not yet material-ized, the wide open possibility, which has not yet been real-ized, the splendid plan, which has not yet been carried out. Such things are of necessity ambiguous. Promising and frag-ile and threatening is the preliminary, which may go forth into all kinds of directions, but of whose arrival one can never be certain.

If one were to suppose that there exists a moment in his-tory, the history of the individual and of all humanity, that is like a first beginning, full of incalculable possibilities and promises, a beginning that hides everything mysteriously within it, and if this beginning of inexpressible, eternal origins carries with it the certainty of its own realization, its own vic-tory, being at once already both promise and fulfillment, then one would have to call this moment in time "holy night": night, because it is a beginning; holy night, because it is a blessed and invincible beginning. One would have to call such a beginning holy night, blessed night.

Therefore we call tonight's celebration Blessed Night, Holy Night. And we sing "Silent Night, Holy Night." Every-where in the world voices are raised in song for this celebration. And it is no coincidence that during the fourth century the date for this celebration was set at a time of the year when even in nature the sun appears to be starting its course anew. Back then the feast of the rising of the "sun of justice," as the prophet calls the Savior, was set on the day of the pagan "*natalis solis invicti*," the feast of the birth of the "invincible god of the sun."

And justly so. For this hour is the holy night. And it is about this night that the Christian faith says: There was its start. There it was that God himself quietly stepped out of the terrible splendor that God inhabits as God and Lord and came to us; quietly he stepped into the small abode of our earthly existence, in the form of a human being. He started out the way we start out, completely poor, completely vulnerable, completely childlike and mild, completely helpless. He who is the infinite, distant future, which we can never catch up with from our end because it appears to continually recede into ever farther distances as soon as we try to meet it on the stony streets of our life, he himself has come toward us, arrived at our end, because otherwise we would not have found our way to him. He has walked with us our path to himself so the path will lead to a blessed ending, because this ending has become also our beginning. God is near; his eternal word of mercy is here, where we are. It is on pilgrimage on our own paths, it tastes of our joy and of our sorrow, it lives our life and dies our death. It has mildly and quietly embedded its own eternal life into this world and into this world's death. It has delivered us by having shared our fate. It has made our beginning its own, stepped onto our path of destiny and opened up this path into the eternal realm of God. And because it has irreversibly accepted us, because the word of God never stops being human, this beginning, which is ours and this world's, a beginning of indestructible promises, this quiet beginning is a Holy Blessed Night.

From this we can also see how we need to celebrate Christmas: as a mystery of holy night. Our celebration has to be still, collected, and soft in our heart, unreservedly open like the heart of a child, which does not yet resist any of the possibilities of its existence but is open to all of them without reserve. The concealed, the wide, and unreachable of our existence must be allowed to quietly hold sway over us, just like the night, which removes from sight that which can be handled and measured and brings up close that which is far away without hemming it in. We have to dare to allow this stillness of the night to come inside us by giving up the escape route into activity, talk, and pretense, the escape route by which we seek to run away from ourselves and from the mystery facing us, the awesome mystery of a never-ending love that frightens us because of our lack of experience with it. We should not desecrate this holy night, this night in which our own life also is consecrated, through cheap holiday activity. The familiar, the childlikeness of this feast, which is quite fitting for such a day, should remain transparent for the unspeakable mystery that introduces a deep intimacy between people and gifts them with the promise of eternal youth. Only the one who allows the multitude of things and people and ambition, obstructing the view to eternity, to recede into the background in the silence of a gentle self-restraint, of detached self-surrender in the silent night of one's own heart; only the one who allows the earthly lights to go out at least for a little while, because they obstruct the view of the stars in heaven; only the one who allows himself or herself to be addressed in the silent night of the heart by the unspeakable, wordless nearness of God, which speaks by its very silence to those who have ears, only such a person will celebrate Christmas the way it ought to be celebrated and keep it from becoming a mere worldly holiday.

We should feel as if on a clear winter night we were stepping beneath the heavenly tent. In the distance we can still glimpse the light of human proximity and familiar comfort, but above us rises heaven and we sense the silent night, which at other times might seem to us ominous and frightening, but which now appears as the silent closeness of the eternal mystery of our existence, which is at once both cradling love and wide expanse.

It is Holy Night! The eternal future has arrived here in our own time. Its gleam is so blinding that we assume it is night. But at any rate it is a blessed night, a night that already has been made warm and bright, that has been made beautiful, familiar, and comforting by the eternal day that it bears hidden within it. It is silent, holy night. But it is this for us only if we allow the holy silence of the night into our innermost being, where our heart is silently awake. We can actually do this quite easily, for such solitude and silence are easy. Such solitude and silence carry only the kind of heaviness that is characteristic of all noble things that are both simple and great. After all, we *are* alone, for in our heart there is an interior landscape of solitude, a place where no one but God can reach. This innermost, separate chamber in our heart exists. The question is only whether we avoid going there on account of an ignorant, guilt-ridden fear based on the fact that no one and nothing from among the earthly familiar may enter there or accompany us on our way to it.

Let us enter there in silence! Let us close the door behind us! Let us listen to the wordless melody that rings through the silence of this night. The silent and solitary soul sings here its most quiet and devout song to the God of the heart. And the soul can be confident that God hears it. For this song no longer has to look for the beloved God beyond the stars in that inaccessible light that God inhabits and on account of which no one can see him. Since it is Christmas and since the Word has become flesh, God is near and and the most subtle word in the quietest chamber of the heart, the word of love finds his ear and his heart. And the one who has retreated into the heart hears there in its depths, despite the night and in the midst of its silence, God's quiet word of love. One has to calm down, not be afraid of the night, and become quiet. Otherwise one will hear nothing. For that which is ultimate can now be spoken only in the silence of the night which, through the merciful arrival of the word into the night of our life, has become blessed night, holy night, silent night.

GRACE IN HUMAN DEPTHS

An Editorial on Christmas

It is not particularly enjoyable to prepare a commentary or to write an editorial about Christmas. The listener or reader may feel the same way. Isn't it always the same old thing—a little "festive mood," some pious and altruistic phrases, a few expensive gifts (along with the work of expressing one's gratitude afterwards)? And then everything continues as before. Those who are Christians are under a particular obligation not to be deluded by the wonder of Christmas. After all, Christians should not be people who cover up the miserable truth about human existence; most certainly not. Christians hang on the wall a cross that frames their life, a cross that is a sign of faith, a gallows of sorts, on which a person who was nailed to it died. Therefore, Christmas can mean only the beginning of a life that in this world ends with a cross (or with death, or in the empty bitterness of complete disappointment—it all comes out the same in the end).

After Christmas—and this should be mentioned during Christmas—everything continues the same as before. We continue the same as before. We reach heavenly heights by doing so: all the way to the moon and farther still. And finally we reach death (though a well-mannered person from either the East or the West should not talk about that because it is not proper, because talking about it is unacceptable unless one is referring to sensational news of human interest, news that could be financially lucrative).

Should one stubbornly withdraw during these days or should one steel oneself to go along with Christmas because it is the best thing to do and proper behavior means not showing how one really feels? Well, aside from these two options, one could do something else, namely ask onself what Christmas actually means from a Christian perspective. An answer to this question might also be of interest to the non-Christian. One could ask whether on the very inside of a person (regardless of whether that person is officially a Christian or not) there lies the invincible courage to believe in Christmas, in the true Christmas, regardless of whether one admits to it or simply says one cannot do so.

Since God made Christmas without asking us, it is quite possible that we believe more than we might like to admit, more than we know based on our theoretical views about ourselves and our life. Why so? We are always those who are beyond themselves (what a burden and what an honor!), the free ones, the ones accountable to themselves, the hoping ones. We live the concreteness of life from the perspective of the transcendent. We have our origin in the depths of the nameless and inexpressible.

We can most certainly act dead with regard to this; we can say that we cannot relate; we can try to stick to the everyday and the concrete, assessing what is held up to the light while refusing to turn to the elusive light (which incidentally is the reason we can see at all what we hold up to the light). Yet the mystery still permeates our existence and repeatedly forces us to look at it: in the joy that is no longer aware of its cause; in fear, which dissolves our ability to comprehend our existence; in the love that knows itself as unconditional and everlasting; in the question that frightens us with its unconditional nature and boundless vastness.

In this way, we are ever confronted with the mystery that is, that is eternal, that is origin without beginning, that is ever present and ever retreats untouched. We call it God. When we say God, we mean the ultimate mystery. When we are aware of the difference between the ability to think compared to the thought itself, joy compared to what is momentarily joyous, responsibility compared to that for which one takes responsibility, the infinite future compared to the present moment, the immeasurable hope compared to the immediate striving, there we are dealing with God, regardless of whether we use this name for the nameless one or another name or none at all.

And when we have accepted this thinking, loving, hoping existence in the depth of our being, despite all the premature, impatient grievances and protests on the surface of our existence, then we have already opened up and given into him. Many will do so, even if they assume they do not know God (one can always know him as the incomprehensible one, for otherwise one has confused him with something else), even if quiet awe prevents them from daring to utter his name.

With such an acceptance of one's existence, an obedient entrusting of oneself to this mystery, it is possible that there occurs what in Christian terminology is called grace: God is and remains mystery. But God also is the depths where human existence is accepted; a nearness and not only distance, forgiveness and not only judgment. God personally fills the never-ending questions of thought, the vastness of hope, and the eternal demand for love. While remaining silent, God is in that depth of our being which opens up to us only when we humbly allow ourselves to be embraced by mystery without wishing to take charge of it. If this happens, then Christmas has already happened in us, this arrival of God, which Christianity says happens by God's grace, which is granted to those who do not resist it on account of a guilt that pairs fear with arrogant self-sufficiency.

Since we are a people of history, of the concrete, of the here and now, and since the arrival of God had to be *his* act, irreversible, irresistible, and historically concrete both as a self-offering of God and as an act to be ultimately accepted by humans, humanity has fixed in its annals this event of the arrival of God as something final, unsurpassable, and irrevocable, namely in Jesus of Nazareth. In him there exists the human act of surrender to the infinite mystery par excellence, and—like everything that involves freedom and decision—is grace in and of itself. In him, God expressed himself (and continues to do so) as the unutterable mystery, as the total and irrevocable word, spoken to all of us as a God of nearness, of inexpressible intimacy and forgiveness.

Here question and answer are united, unblended and inseparable; here God and the human being are one without mutual exclusion.

Even when people are still far from using explicit words for this type of revelation yet are accepting of their life, of their humanity, in silent patience or, better yet, in faith, hope, and love (or whatever one might call these) as the mystery hidden in the secret of eternal love and as bearing life in the very midst of death, then they are saying "yes" to Jesus Christ, even though they may be unaware of it. For when people let go and jump, they fall into an already existing depth, even if they did not personally measure that depth beforehand. If they accept their own humanity (though that is terribly difficult, and it remains unknown whether one ever really does so), they have accepted the Son of Man, since in him God has accepted humanity.

According to scripture, whoever loves his neighbor has fulfilled the law. This is the ultimate truth, because God himself has become the neighbor, and in every neighbor it is always this one Neighbor and most Distant One whom one accepts and loves. When we accept the silent mystery that envelops our existence and appears as both distance and overwhelming nearness, the sheltering home and the mild love that does not hold back anything; when we have the courage to see ourselves in a way made possible only by grace and faith; when we recognize the reason for this closeness and its absolute promise and arrival in the one whom we call the Son of Man, then we have experienced Christmas by the grace of faith.

Some may have the courage of an explicit faith in the truth of Christmas, while others accept it only quietly in the unfathomable depth of their own existence, filled by a blessed hope without words. When the former accept the latter as "anonymous" Christians, then all can celebrate Christmas together. The seemingly superficial and conventional Christmas hoopla is blessed in the end with truth and depth. What looks like a sham in light of all the holiday activity, then, is not the complete truth, for in the background stands the holy and silent truth that God has arrived after all and is celebrating Christmas with us.

Thus, we are more honestly and more deeply in the truth when we are able to look beyond the initial and justified skepticism about the conventional Christmas by celebrating it freely, not taking too seriously our doubts, and rejoicing in the feast as the sign that God's arrival has already transcended all our plans and all our disappointments. If then after Christmas things continue the same as before, the truth still remains that God has accepted us. And our depths are filled by his grace.

THE ARRIVAL OF GOD INTO A LOCKED-UP WORLD
On the Feast of St. Stephen

Today, on this second day of Christmas, the church celebrates in its liturgy St. Stephen, a deacon and the first martyr of the early church in Jerusalem. He was stoned in about the year AD 35, soon after Jesus' death and resurrection. One hears of Stephen in Acts 6 and 7. The reason he is remembered today is that in the fourth century the Eastern church decided that December 26 was to be his feast day. This decision was made before the Western church's celebration of Christmas on December 25 had become known in the East. It means that Stephen had no chance to walk to the manger, but that, instead, the manger walked to him when, by the fifth century, St. Stephen's Day, which comes from the East, was linked to Christmas Day in the West.

Thus, the connection of St. Stephen's Day with Christmas is a historical coincidence; it was not planned. But even historical coincidences can have some good and deep meaning, often more so than things that have been purposely designed or planned. Therefore, let this young hero continue to stand with a palm frond by the manger of the child bedded on straw. Stephen fits well here, because if we consider what scripture tells us about his unique life and death, then we can definitely hear a Christmas-like message, unless, of course, we misunderstand Christmas.

Stephen is a man of faith and of the Holy Spirit (Acts 6:5), of grace and power (Acts 6:8). He is a person of freedom and, one might even say, of a courage that dares to move about, to venture out of the merely customary, away from the firm fences of the letter of the law. This is why he predicts the destruction of the temple, knowing—like the apostle Paul yet even before Paul himself does—about Jesus' overcoming the institutionalization of Old Testament tradition (Acts 6:14). In the speech of Acts 7 Stephen sees the entire history of the salvation and the destruction of his people as a singular pilgrimage, a constant departure, a crossing into the unknown, a sending forth in which someone is called by and to the eternal mystery—the true mystery, not the tangible idol that we ourselves create and carry ahead of us as our guiding light on a journey filled with deception. Because this is the way Stephen feels, he is open to faith in his people's future, a future that he experiences in the present, open to the arrival of the Messiah and hence to the message of Christmas. Because this is the way he feels, he cannot but interpret holistically the history of destruction, which parallels the history of salvation, as an open movement, as a resistance to the prophets, "who prophesy about the coming of the Righteous One," as a resistance the climax of which is the devious murder of him who has become the aim of this movement (Acts 7:52ff). And when Stephen dies, he dies unto the open, unto the infinite limitlessness of his blessed spiritual existence, and he sees precisely in this infinite moment the one who stands there, who has come near in order to bridge the infinite distance; who has come so as to make the world as a whole the dwelling place of God, who dissolves the idolatry of the world and its powers by himself being the incarnate presence of God among us: I see the heavens opened and the Son of Man standing at the right hand of God! (Acts 7:56).

Is this youth, who stands by the manger with a palm frond of victory, not a good interpreter of Christmas? Christmas is the arrival of God into the self-enclosure of the world, so that the world can open up to God and the heavens open out to the world. Christmas says: The movement of the world has reached its destination because the aim of this searching, ever newly departing movement of history has been reached; but this aim has only now become revealed to the world in the form of God's own life. We hold up before our eyes the idols of our utopias and think that we can move toward them as our aim; in the meantime, we encounter only our own aimlessness, meaninglessness, and finality; we become lost in dead ends. As Stephen says in his sermon, we make idols for ourselves, idols to lead us (Acts 7:40). But they lead us only because we put them in front of our eyes and carry them, thereby projecting ourselves with our questionable sense of direction into the wall of dark emptiness toward which we are headed. Of course, how could we accept a destination that was not ultimately leading us back to ourselves? And yet, how can we approve of a destination where we could find *only* ourselves? What is there to say? We want to find ourselves and yet are not enough for ourselves; we have to have both—ourselves and eternity— all wrapped into one.

If we call ourselves human beings and we call eternity God, we can say what our aim should be, if it exists: the God-person. Now Christmas says: The destination has arrived, sent from God, and now look, it is the seeking one and the eternal sought-after in one person. It is the Son of Man, the God-person, the splendor of God that one can now behold, but only when one sees Jesus standing at the right hand of God. The destination has by its own accord moved toward the seeker and taken up the seeker into that which is sought after, so that the seeker no longer will be lost by seeking after the other, so that the seeker becomes the one who finds by simply being the purely seeking one, the one who seeks, the one who naturally wants to be found by God and does not simply revel in self in the fleeting aimlessness of movement that is actually no seeking at all. Whoever looks at pure openness and does not confuse it with the concrete figure; whoever is willing to accept the here-and-now and everywhere-and-always as one and the same, not just as a casual and abstract theory, but con-cretely in life; whoever finds the One in this way and because of it; whoever accepts this unity of God and human being in the history of humanity, namely in Jesus Christ—this person has found while seeking, has arrived while still in motion, not because the One is humanly speaking both, but because God has found the seeker. When we accept ourselves completely the way we are, when we accept what we have become because the word of God has become flesh and has turned our darkness into Christmas, then we find what we are looking for. Then, in true Christmas fashion, the heavens are opened for us in the same way as they were for Stephen and we can see in faith the splendor of God because we see standing there victoriously the human Son, the infinite human being. Truly, ever since the first Christmas, the heavens have been open because heaven has come down to earth. The believer sees God and God looks back with a human face and loves with a human heart. Since then, the infinite has drawn near and the finite has opened up into the infinite.

NEW YEAR AND EPIPHANY

SPIRITUAL ACCOUNT OF A YEAR

Today is the last day of the year. Therefore, it is appropriate to say good-bye to the year in a Christian way. One can truly do so only individually, for each person is quite different from the next, and so each year one lives differs from that of another. God guides each person individually. And this God is not someone who, lacking in ideas, needs to give even once to one person the same as to another, because as creator and lord of our life, God has an eternal dimension that contains an unforeseeable wealth of possibilities to be dispensed.

And still, the year of one person is also the same as that of the next. For in each case, a year has gone by. That at least is the same. We say farewell to a year that has passed. We do so together, in our churches, in the community of the one blessed body. We leave behind one year. We leave behind its many days, its work, its worries, its disappointments, its hardships, the plans that we may have made during its course and that have not materialized, or at least not in the way we had hoped. We leave the year behind with our guilt, with our failures, in short, with all that our poor hearts have made of it.

To whom do we return the year to which we say good-bye, the year we are leaving behind? Is it even possible to give it to somebody? Has it not simply dissolved into a state in which it is no more? Only because we are saying good-bye to it and it is no longer available to us for daily, even hourly, decision-making

29

does not mean that it is extinguished and no more. On the contrary: From a Christian perspective, from God's perspective, from our own perspective as spiritual beings who belong to eternity, we would have to say that the past year is the one gained, the one retained, the one no longer reversible, the one that remains. Whether the years ahead of us will be ours is known only to God and not to us. But to us belongs the past, and it is quite permissible for us Christians to say that. Still, we can hope and pray that God will grant us much more of the future in this our life, which is eternal, so that the future also may become ours eventually and, when it has seemingly gone by, it will remain as well.

And who preserves for us the past, the remaining, the irretrievable year? God does. God has entered it in what scripture calls "the book of life." He knows this year, and before him it remains present. He has entered it into the book of life, which is who *we* are in our spiritual substance, in the historical and spiritual characteristics that we have irretrievably imprinted upon ourselves during our life, and hence also during the past year. Since thereby this past year remains present, we can still make it into what it is supposed to be during our hour of saying good-bye.

Let us say good-bye to the old year with gratitude, so that it can still become what it is supposed to be, the gift of the grace of God. For God has given to us every single day of the year. And if we have truly accepted those days as given to us by God's love (and there is still time for doing so), then they were blessed days, days of grace and of salvation. We should never think of ourselves as so ill-willed, bitter, skeptical, gruff, or negative that such thinking transforms itself into a skeptical attitude toward God. If we were to say that we had been poor and inadequate, that we had been burdened, tired, fearful, meeting neither life's demands nor God's call, we might be saying something right perhaps. But if as Christians we were to say that about ourselves and about our past year, then we would be unfair to God. Did God not preserve us by his grace? Did God not give us the

blessed body of his Son? Is not God's Holy Spirit in our hearts?
Did we not carry God's burden throughout this year, despite
our sweat and our groans? Did not God's grace speak through
us to others? (One should not say that the good done easily is
in God's eyes any less true grace, even if one were to admit that
the good involving great difficulty often or frequently did not
get done by us, unless God extracted it from us through life's
harshness.) Did we not venture into much that seemed hard
and yet accept it, despite grumbling and protest, which means
that—even if we did not give this much thought—we accepted
God, since one can accept what is death-dealing with a truly
welcoming attitude only by reaching for true and eternal life?
If we had not done so, we would not be stepping before God
right now, on this last evening of the year, and we would not be
able to look back at this year and bless it.

But since the year was made possible by God's grace the
way we experienced it, since it was more God's merciful doing
than our failure, we can bless it, we are permitted to do so and
have to do so. We may say good-bye to this year with gratitude
and place it into the hands of a gracious and loving God, the
God who is eternity and who preserves for us our part of eternity, including the part to which we say good-bye today and
tomorrow. What we offer in gratitude God graciously takes,
and what is taken by God is preserved and made holy, blessed,
and set free. With that it remains eternal: our year is saved and
forever retained.

And then we move on, taking with us from this past year
ourselves, with our former responsibilities, our old concerns,
our old burdens and worries, along with our old fear, which
also lingers somewhere in our soul, and the sense that we are
beggars who must continue to ask for God's forgiveness and
for bread and the strength to manage day after day.

And though we have no way of foreseeing the new year as
we say good-bye to the old, we can gladly bring ourselves into
the new. We bring ourselves the way we are because we are
creatures of God the eternal Father and the creation of his

hands. God has made us and takes responsibility for what he has created. He takes responsibility for the history of this world and even for every single person's life. He has enveloped us in his grace, his love, and his faithfulness. When we bring with us into the new year our past and our worries, with all our foibles and weariness, our faithful and merciful God goes with us. And the burden we continue to carry into the new year will not be more than we can bear. Even if it were to oppress us, God would still fully and gladly receive us. And what might look like the final pain and the ultimate suffering would only be an ultimate unburdening and an entry into the incomprehensible life of God.

We do not carry more than we are capable of carrying. When we have the impression that only the burdens of the old year carry over into the new while what was easy and joyous is left behind, then let us say during our good-bye to the old year: "My God, you are coming along, and therefore I gladly carry with me all of the old year that I simply cannot leave behind, recognizing it as yours, to be preserved for life eternal."

So, let us say good-bye to the past year! It was a year of the Lord, a year of grace, a year of inner growth, even if we did not feel it. After all, God's strength achieves victory in our weakness. Thus, we really can praise God at the end of the year and thank him and give him honor, for he is good and his mercy is everlasting.

IN THE NAME OF JESUS
Luke 2:21

We are starting a new year in secular life, not in the life of the church. But the earthly year, the everyday year during which we live out our lives of work and worry is the arena in which our salvation through God takes place. Thus, we have every reason to also begin this year in the name of the

Lord. So, let us start "in God's name" and continue, honestly and undeterred! Time flies. One could become despondent or nostalgic during the New Year's celebration since yet another piece of this earthly existence has gone by irretrievably. But in reality time flies toward God and his eternity, not into the past and toward destruction. Therefore: in God's name.

On the feast of the Three Wise Men, it is religious tradition to write the names of C + M + B (Caspar, Melchior, and Balthasar) above the entry way. In the same way, let us write the name of God above the new year, the name of the God in whom is our help, the name of Jesus. Jesus means "Yahweh is helping." Yahweh was the proper name for God among the covenant people of the Old Testament. It is possible to give God a name, even though God is nameless and unfathomable and people ultimately know God only as distant and hidden and incomprehensible. Yet, God can have a name because God revealed himself in the history of his actions and speech, so that we can see how exactly he wants to relate to us. All the experiences that people have had with the living God on account of God's dealings with humans are summed up in the "name" they give God.

Only a proper name, never a merely abstract term, describes the full, indivisible, and intrinsic sum total of what one can know about a living person with whom one has regular dealings. And Jesus as a proper name tells us how this Yahweh wishes to be toward us: near, loving, helping, faithful to the end. Through and by Jesus—and by no one and nothing else—we know who we have in God. Jesus is the word of the Father, in whom God speaks as a word of mercy. And if we want to say who our God is, we will have to call him Jesus. If we were to forget this word, God would disappear from us into the dark distance, the abyss of incomprehensibility. But we Christians know the ultimate name of God: Jesus. For that is the name given to the child who is God, the eternal youth of the world, a human being and thus the eternal face of God.

So let us give the same name to this coming year! Let us mark the cross of this Jesus on our forehead, spirit, and heart!

Let us say without hesitation: Our help is in the name of the Lord! And then let us confidently cross the threshold of the new year. Where *his* name shines, there even the darkest hour of the year will be an hour of the Lord and his salvation.

ABOUT THE BLESSED JOURNEY
OF THOSE LOOKING FOR GOD
Epiphany

During these last days of Christmas, all of us have probably celebrated quite a few feasts, for our own benefit or for that of others. We were joyous or maybe only quiet and collected or perhaps even a bit nostalgic, since it is not always easy to be in a festive mood. But at least things were a little less ordinary and our hearts were a little lighter during these child-friendly days—days that were friendly also for the child in our own hearts—a time during which we could consider things that lie beyond the everyday.

At the end of this festive season is the feast of the appearance of the Lord. Actually, it is another Christmas, the Christmas that during the fourth century traveled from the Eastern church to ours and was put right next to ours, which is celebrated on December 25. It is the feast of the announcement and revelation of the Savior and redeemer of all people, not just his own people but also the Gentiles and everyone in the world. It is the feast that says: "Made manifest is the grace and benevolence toward all people by our God and Savior Jesus Christ." It is the feast that says: See, God is here, silent, quiet, the way spring is contained in the small seed, certain of its own victory, hidden beneath the wintry earth and already more powerful than all darkness and all cold. It is the feast that says: God is here. God has become human, has entered into the poverty and smallness of our life, and has loved us so much

that he has become one of us, so that there will never be any
doubt about how the drama that humanity is acting out on the
stage of its history will end, so that it is certain—by a blessed
faith—that this so seemingly meaningless and improvised
tragedy of blood and tears is still a divine comedy full of heavenly purpose, because God is no longer only watching but
rather playing a role in it himself and speaking the decisive
lines. It is the feast of the appearance of the Lord, in which is
still celebrated Christmas Eve, the Holy Night that is brighter
than our dark days because it has welcomed the eternal little
light of our own darkness.

Nevertheless, there is one aspect of Christmas that is more
evident in this second feast than in the first. Not only did God
come to us but by the power of his divine deed we ourselves
have been set in motion, we ourselves are moving toward the
one who has come to us. After all, we refer to this feast, this
"high feast" as it was called during the Middle Ages, as the
feast of the Wise Men or of the Three Kings. The latter name
may sound un-theological and unhistorical, given the fact that
scripture specifies neither that the wise men from the Orient
were kings nor that there were three of them; still, the feast of
"Three Kings" points us in a significant way to the secret of
the feast, namely, that the first people coming from far away
were looking for the path in the midst of many obstacles, wandering about and journeying to the child who was their savior.
Therefore, this day is the feast of the blessed pilgrimage of
people who are looking for God while on their journey
through life and the feast of those who find God because they
have been looking for him.

In the first twelve verses of the second chapter of
Matthew—the story of the magi from faraway Babylon who,
while being led by the star, had traveled through deserts and
had, despite the indifference and the politics they encountered, found the child eventually, so that they could worship
him as the savior king—we truly are reading our own story, the
story of our own pilgrimage.

Is it not true that all of us are pilgrims, people without a fixed home, even if we have never had to leave home? Time flies, days go by, and we are ever in the process of changing, ever moving on. Somewhere and somehow we began the journey and suddenly we find ourselves on the way, a way that keeps moving us forward and never returns to the same place. The journey takes us through childhood, through the strength of youth and the maturity of age, through a few feast days and a lot of common days, through highs and lows, through innocence and guilt, through love and disappointment, ever and invariably taking us from the Orient of life to the Occident of death. And it continues invariably and relentlessly, so that often we are unaware of it and assume that we are standing still; at least it seems that way, because while we are moving, everything else around us is also moving along with us.

But where does the journey lead? The moment we became aware of our existence, was it like finding ourselves sitting on a moving train without any idea of where it was headed, so that all we needed to do was settle down and act in the right and proper way but never ask where this train was going? Or, while traveling, were we looking for a destination because deep inside our hearts we knew that such a destination exists, regardless of how hard it is to get there and how far away it may be? Is human life only the place where the world experiences most intensely its own absurdity? Does our spirit rise only to realize with great pain that it has come from a dark abyss of nothing in order to fall back there, to disappear like a shooting star that on its dark path through space momentarily lights up upon entering the atmosphere? Are we on the journey only to end up getting lost? Is it not permissible for the heart and the mind to ask about the train's destination, regardless of whether the answer is only a silent, hopeless shaking of the head? Is it not permitted to ask? Who would hinder the heart from doing so?

We already know the answers to these questions: God is the name of our journey's destination. And God lives far away. The journey there may seem too far for us and too difficult.

We may also be unclear as to what we mean by the word "God": ground of all being, sea to which all the waters of our longing flow, the nameless beyond that lives behind all that is familiar, the unsolvable riddle containing all others and preventing us from finding their ultimate solution in the familiar and tangible, the boundless vastness in the purest simplicity of reality, truth, light, life, and love. Toward him is directed the flight of all creation throughout time and through all transition and change. Would it not make sense for our own poor heart to get up and seek him, given that the free spirit is bound to find what it seeks and given that God has promised—has given his word—that he will permit himself to be found by those who are looking for him? By grace, God does not want to be merely what lies ever before the traveler, but is the one who wants to be found, found in a way that is eye-to-eye, heart-to-heart, found by the creature with the eternal heart, the one we call the human being.

Just look and see: The magi have set out, their hearts traveling to God even as their feet take them to Bethlehem. They are looking for him, and because they are, he also guides them. They are those longing for the Savior out of a hunger and thirst for justice. They believe that people can ill afford not to make the first step simply because God would have to make a thousand in order for us to meet. They are looking for God, for salvation in the heavens and in the heart. They are looking for him in solitude and among others, even among the Jews and in their holy writings. They see a star strangely rising in the sky. And, out of sheer mercy, God permits even their astrology, foolish as it may be, to prove useful, since their innocent hearts know no better. It is likely that their hearts tremble a bit when both the theory of the Jewish messianic expectation of which they vaguely knew and the theory of their astrology suddenly converge in the form of a very concrete journey. They probably are a little frightened by their own courage and would have preferred that their noble principles of theoretical reasoning had not ended up looking so surreal and unpractical.

But suddenly, having left their homeland and having courageously taken a leap into uncertainty, their hearts grow light; it is the lightness of risking everything and being more courageous by common standards than one really is. They walk on meandering paths, but from God's perspective the paths are straight because these men are looking for God out of faith. They are afraid to be so far from the familiar, but they know that everyone is ever in progress and has to be ever departing anew to find home, the home that is more than a tent by the road. They know from life experience (which is more than the theory of reason) that to live means to change and to be perfect means to have changed much. That is how they walk. The journey is long, the feet frequently tired, the heart often heavy and distraught. And the poor heart feels strange and pained to be so different from the hearts of other people, who are so seriously and foolishly immersed in their everyday affairs and look at these wandering travelers with pity and dismay over what seems to be such a uselessly squandered journey. But the heart perseveres, uncertain of where the strength is coming from, certain only that it does not come from oneself, that it ever suffices, that it never ceases as long as one does not ask or look daringly into the heart's hollow container to see if anything is left, and as long as one continues drawing with courage on its secret contents.

Hearts such as these cannot be intimidated. They do not look down upon those they pass. But they do pass them by, thinking: One day, in his own good time, he will be calling them too; but we, for our part, are not allowed to lose faith in the light only because others cannot see it yet. The magi obtain information, gruffly given by the scribes in Jerusalem, and receive a wily order from the king. But their ears hear only a heavenly message because their hearts are good and full of longing. And when they arrive and kneel down, they are doing only what they have been doing all along on their search and their journey: they offer up the gold of their love, the incense of their respect, and the myrrh of their pain before the invisibly visible God. Then, their path leads them once again away from the country in which the holy story took place. As quietly as they came, they disappear from our ken (just as those who die). But those who have just once given their entire heart selflessly to the star have already risked everything and prevailed. What great joy! There were royal hearts in these men that have now gone. Even if their true journey to the invisible, eternal light continues still and perhaps only just began when they arrived back home, hearts like theirs, royal hearts like theirs, have a way of reaching their destination. Therefore, we can call these men from the East happy.

Let us go on this adventurous journey of the heart toward God the way they did! Let us not forget what lies behind us. Everything is still future. All possibilities of life are still open because we are still in the process of finding God, of finding more of him. Nothing is over or lost to those who walk toward God, whose smallest reality is bigger than our most daring dreams, the God who is eternal youthfulness and whose nature does not know dismay.

We are walking through deserts. But you, heart, do not be dismayed at the sight of the train of pilgrims and people who are moving along, bent over by the burden of their hidden pain, ever moving and apparently headed in one single direction without aim. Do not be dismayed, heart, for the star is here and shines. The holy writings are clear about where the Savior is to be found. The restless longing spurs on. Look at it yourself: Is there not the star in the firmament of your heart? It may be small or it may be far away. But it is there. It is small only because you are far away from it. It is far away only because you have been sent on an eternal journey. But the star is there. This star is also a longing for freedom inside, for goodness, for blessedness, for the ability to feel remorse over one's own weakness and sinfulness. Why are you putting clouds in front of the star: the clouds of dismay, of disappointment, of bitterness over failure, the clouds of mocking or negative words about lost dreams for a blessed hope? Stop resisting, because the star is shining. Whether you make it the star of your journey or not, there it is on your horizon, and even your ill-will and weakness will not extinguish it.

So, why should we not trust and go? Why should we not look to the star in the firmament of our hearts? Why should we not follow the light? Only because there are people like the scribes in Jerusalem who know the way to Bethlehem but are not going there? Only because there are kings like Herod who see the news about the Messiah only as a disruption of their political plans, kings who even today are after the life of this child? Only because most people stay home in cynical pride and think that such venturesome travels of the heart are foolish? Let them be, while we follow the star of the heart!

And in what way is the heart to travel? It will have to be on the move. It is the heart that prays, that seeks, that shyly but honestly practices doing good, that moves, that moves toward God; it is the heart that believes and does not turn bitter, the heart that views the foolishness of kindness as smarter than the cleverness of selfish ambition, the heart that believes in the goodness of God, the heart that wants to allow itself to be lovingly forgiven by God (which is much harder to do than one might think), that allows itself to be confronted with its own secret unbelief and is not surprised by it but admits to it while praising God. Such a heart has begun the venturesome journey toward God in the company of all other royal hearts.

A new year has begun. During this year too, all paths lead from the Orient to the Occident across the deserts of a life that is by its very nature transient. And one can have here also the experience of a pilgrimage toward that which is absolute, namely God. So, dear heart, get up and walk! The star is shining. There is not much to take along for the journey. And much will get lost along the way. But let it go. The gold of love, the frankincense of longing, the myrrh of pain you already have. He will take them. And we will find.

LENT

LENT: MY NIGHT KNOWS NO DARKNESS

Even today, the liturgical year of the church has a time dedicated to penance. Does this not seem strange? We certainly understand that in former centuries such a time was considered necessary for the management of the spiritual and the religious life. People back then were full of life's joy, satisfied and carefree, and they celebrated Mardi Gras in the streets and laughed the laughter that still came from the heart. Therefore, they could presumably experience a brief period of recollection, of contemplative seriousness, and of ascetic restraint from life's luxuries as a beneficial change from everyday life and for the good of the soul.

What about us? Do we not consider the proclamation of the church about the start of a time of seriousness, contemplation, and fasting as something strangely surreal, and do we not see a "time of fasting" as a slightly dusty ceremony left over from the good old days? How is such a time relevant for us today with our many needs, our hopelessness with regard to this world, our bitter hearts, our sense that we would be willing to fast as long as it did not mean going hungry?

1

In the present time our fasting, our Lenten season, starts long before Ash Wednesday... and will continue far beyond the forty days until Easter. It is a time so real that during this liturgically set period of penance we need not use this time as a convenient occasion for sentimentality, as is done in political speeches. The non-liturgical time of our present Lenten life looks harder and more difficult to us than any period of deprivation in generations past. Yes, we are suffering to some degree from a need to be filled and the absence of a carefree, safe life, as well as from the fact that we sit in darkness and in the shadow of death; however, mostly—if one dare say so—we are suffering from a sense that God is far away. God is distant from us.

This is not a statement that is true for everyone. It is not a statement that should trouble those hearts that are full of God. But it also is not a statement saying that people can at least take pride in their ability to experience the infinite through the bitterness of their hearts. It is not a statement that promotes a human trait that should never be lost or that God should make sure to preserve in order to give us his nearness and the certainty of his blessed love, as if desperation could enlarge the human heart more than happiness. To declare one's distance from God a noble human trait (as do some interpretations of human existence that call themselves existential philosophy) is sinful and stupid and perverse. Such a distance from God in many people is a fact and demands an explanation; it is a sorrow, the deepest sorrow of our Lenten life for as long as we journey apart from the Lord.

Distance from God does not mean here that a person is denying God's existence or indifferently ignoring it in life. Such an understanding is often, though not always, a wrong interpretation of the state that is meant here. Rather, distance from God here means something that can equally, if not mostly, exist in those who believe in God, long for God, and look for God's light and sanctifying nearness. Even believers— and they especially—can and often are made to experience the fact that God appears as someone rather unreal, that God is mute and silently rejecting, as if he were framing our existence only as an empty, distant horizon in whose labyrinth of infinity our thoughts and the desires of our hearts are utterly lost. Distance from God says that our spirit has grown tired of the unsolved riddles, that our spirit has grown despondent over the unanswered prayers, and that we are tempted to see "God" only as one of those ultimate yet untrustworthy affirmations under which people repeatedly hide their own desperation, even though this desperation, too, has lost the strength to take itself seriously. God appears to us only as this bodiless, inaccessible infinity that, to make matters worse, seems to make even more finite and questionable our small piece of existence and makes us feel even more homeless in this world, since it seduces us into a vast longing that we ourselves cannot satisfy and that God seemingly cannot either.

Yes, it appears as if Western people today have to suffer and do penance in the "purgatory" of feeling distant from God more so than people of previous times. If individuals can experience, apart from the blessed moment of feeling close to God, the nights of the spiritual senses where the eternity of the living God draws near by the fact that God appears more distant and inapproachable, why should nations and continents not have similar experiences, so that theirs can somehow become the holy fate of all? The fact that this dismal condition may have been occasioned by the sins of an entire era does not preclude it from being a *felix culpa*, a blessed guilt.

Seen from this angle, the theoretical and practical atheism that many people express today is a wrong, impatient, and one-sided response to such a condition and is reactionary in the truest sense of the word, for it is still a clinging to the rather childlike notion that God needs to be near before worship is possible, and that when such nearness is not present one no longer understands God and can even say that God does not exist. Today's atheism becomes then the willful refusal to mature in the dark purgatory of a debris-covered heart for the sake of the God who is always greater than the God who was perceived and loved the previous day.

But enough of that! The sense of feeling distant from God exists and touches believers and non-believers alike, confuses the mind, and frightens the heart. Believers do not like to admit to it because they think that something like that should not happen to them, despite the fact that their Lord himself cried out: My God, why have you forsaken me? And the others, the non-believers, draw the wrong conclusions from it.

2

Since feeling distant from God in our debris-covered heart is the ultimate bitterness of our life's Lenten season, it is appropriate to ask what can be done about it and, along the same lines, how the church's liturgical season of Lent is to be lived. For when the bitter distance from God turns into holy worship, the Lenten season of the world is transformed into the Lenten season of the church.

The first thing you will need to do is to expose your debris-covered heart to the experience of feeling distant from God by refusing to escape through pious or worldly activity, by enduring the experience without the common sedatives, without committing sin, and without stubborn desperation. When you experience the heart's emptiness like that, what kind of God is it who is actually distant from you? It certainly is not the true and living God, for he is the incomprehensible, the nameless one who is truly the God of your boundless heart. The one distant from you is a god that does not exist: a god that can be comprehended, a god of small ideas and cheap, undemanding human thoughts, a god of earthly security, a god that makes sure that the children do not cry and that human love does not end up in disappointment—in short, a rather dignified idol. That is the god that has become distant. And is not such a god-distance bearable?

Something else is true: You will need to permit your heart to experience this kind of despair, a despair that appears to be robbing you of everything, seemingly blocking your heart's escape out into life, into fulfillment, into the open, into God. Do not despair when experiencing despair: Let the despair take all away from you, since what is taken from you is only the finite, the unimportant, even if it may have been ever so wonderful and great, even if it may be yourself with your ideals, with your smart and detailed plans for your life, with your image of a god that looks more like you than the incomprehensible one. Allow all the exits to be blocked, for they are only exits into the finite and paths into dead ends. Do not be frightened by the solitude and forsakenness in your internal prison, which appears to be as dead as a grave. For if you stand firm, refusing to flee from despair and in the despair over the loss of your former idol that you called God you do not doubt the true God; if you stand firm, which is a true miracle of grace, then you will realize suddenly that your grave-like prison cell is locked up only against what is meaningless and finite, that its deathly emptiness is only the vastness of God's presence, that silence is filled with a word without words by the one who stands above all names and who is all in all. The silence is *his* silence. He is saying that he is here.

And the second thing to do in your despair is to realize that he is here and to understand by faith that he is with you. This means realizing that he has been expecting you for a long time in the deepest dungeon of your debris-covered heart, that he has been silently listening and waiting for a long time to see whether you in the busy din that is called your life might give him a chance to speak, to speak a word that has sounded up until then only like deathly silence. It also means realizing that you will not perish when you release the worry about yourself and for your life, that you will not perish when you let go, that you will not end up in despair when you finally despair of yourself, of your own wisdom and strength, and of the wrong image of God that is being torn away from you.

As if by a miracle that has to happen anew each day, you will realize that you have arrived at him. You will suddenly realize that your sense of being distant from God is in reality only the disappearance of the world, because the dawn of God in your soul has begun; that the darkness is nothing else but the brightness of God that casts no shadow; and that your sense of having no exit is only the immeasurability of God to which no paths are needed because he is already here. You will realize that you should not try to flee from your empty heart by your own strength because he is already here, so that there is no reason to flee from this blessed despair into a solace that would not be solace, because such solace does not exist.

He is here. Do not try to hold onto him. He does not run away. Do not try to make sure he *is* or try touching him with the hands of your greedy heart. You would touch only emptiness, not because he is distant or unreal, but because he is infinity that cannot be touched. He is here, in the midst of your debris-covered heart, he alone. Yet, he who is everything looks as if he were nothing.

Then, all by itself, there comes peace, which is purest activity, silence that is filled with God's word, trust that no longer fears, certainty that no longer needs reassurance, and strength that becomes powerful in weakness, a life rising from death. Then, there is nothing else in us but God and the almost unnoticeable and yet all-pervasive faith that he is, that he is here, and that we are his.

But one thing has yet to be said: This sense of being distant from God would not be the dawn of God in the midst of the dead, debris-covered heart had not the Son of Man, who is the Son of the Father, suffered and experienced the same in his own heart along with us, for us, and before us. Yes, he suffered and experienced all of this. It happened in the garden from whose fruit people wanted to press the oil of gladness but which was in reality the garden of a lost paradise. He lay face-down and death climbed into his living heart, into the heart of the world. The heavens were closed up and the world was like a vast grave in which he alone lay, covered by the guilt and the hopelessness of the world. The angel, who looked like death, handed him for strength the chalice of all bitterness, so that he fell into agony. The earth swallowed darkly and greedily the drops of blood of his deathly fear. But God enclosed everything like the night that no longer promises another day. One could no longer differentiate between God and death. In the seeming boundlessness of the deathly silence, where people dulled their sadness by sleep, there floated somewhere the small voice of the Son, which was the only sign of God's presence that still remained. And it seemed as if this voice, too, might drown in the silence at any moment. But then the great miracle happened: the voice remained. In this small voice that sounded like the voice of a dead person, the Son addressed the awesome God as "Father" and said about his own abandonment: "Your will be done." And then, in an act of unspeakable courage, he commended his abandoned soul into the hands of his Father.

Since then our own poor soul, too, has been placed into the hands of this Father, whose former deadly decree has turned into love. Since then, our despair has been redeemed, the emptiness of our heart has found fulfillment, and our sense of being distant from God has been transformed into a sense of nearness. When, in the weary darkness of our heart, we pray with the Son the prayer he said in the garden and when we do so in simple faith, there will be no storm of delight right away, as if his words were mysteriously rising from somewhere in the depths of our heart and becoming our own. But the prayer will have power enough. Each day, it will be just enough. And it will be for as long as God sees fit. And that is enough. He knows when and where our heart has been sufficiently tested, even here on earth, in order to endure the eventual blinding dawn of its blessedness, the poor heart that now shares by faith in Jesus Christ the night with him and which to the one who believes is nothing but our eyes' blind darkness to the profuse light of God, the holy night when God is first born in our hearts.

All of this should not remain religious lyrics for Sunday pondering. It has to be practiced amidst the burden and bitterness of everyday life. When you begin to practice standing firm and drinking willingly of the chalice in which are contained poverty, need, and the sense of being distant from God, then you will have started a Lent that is blessed. Do you want to try it? Say to the God of your heart who is already near: Grant me your grace.

EASTER

THE BEGINNING OF GLORY

Imagine someone lighting the tip of a fuse in order to set off a huge explosion and then waiting for the explosion to happen, which it certainly will. One would surely not say that the lighting of the fuse is merely an event of the past. The beginning of an event, still in the process of development yet irreversibly and irresistibly moving toward its climax, is not something of the past but of the present, even containing the future; in short, it is a movement that continues because it presently carries in concrete union both the past and the present. We should be clear about that from the start if anything meaningful is to be said about the resurrection of the Lord.

Easter is not the celebration of a past event. The "Alleluia" of Easter is not a reference to something that was, but is the proclamation of a beginning that has already announced the outcome of a most distant future. Resurrection says: Glory has already begun. And that which has begun is in the process of coming to its completion. Will it take a long time? Yes, it will take a few thousand years at least, because that is the "brief" time needed for an incomprehensible sum of reality and history to squeeze through the narrow death pains of an incredible transformation (called natural and world history) and to move on toward its glorious completion. Everything is in motion. Nothing on earth can remain the same. Slowly we realize, or at least sense, that even nature has a single-track history and that it is in progress, in the process of evolving, unfolding in time and with an ever-increasing incomprehensible grandeur, reaching ever higher degrees of reality behind which lies the creative power of God. Slowly we realize also that human history has a single direction and is not the eternal repetition of ever-the-same "under the sun"; that in a certain sequence the nations are called upon to carry out their distinct historical mission; that history as a whole has a shape and a direction that cannot be reversed.

But what is the direction of this movement in nature, history, and spirit? Is everything headed toward a crash beyond which is nothing but meaninglessness and nothingness? Is there movement only for movement's sake? Is everything ultimately a demonstration of the emptiness and vanity of things, which will be unmasked as such in the course of natural and world history, so that all its comedies and tragedies are mere theater, to be taken seriously in their illusory shape only as long as they are in progress and have not yet come to an end?

How far has this history advanced? Has the meaning of the play of history in its indefinite proportions already been determined? Has the final, decisive key word—the word that would make sense out of everything prior to it and would invariably point to how the piece will end—already been spoken?

We Christians say that this entire natural and world history has meaning, a blessed and transfigured meaning, a comprehensive meaning that is no longer diluted by absurdity and darkness, but one that is ultimate reality and unity, comprised of all possibility and glory, which we call God. (Doing so is a way of postulating absolute meaning.) God is the same within as without, the aim of all history. God is in the process of arriving. All the waters of change in the world are flowing toward God, rather than dissipating into meaninglessness and a bottomless nothing. But if we say this and declare eternity as the reference point of the temporal, eternity as the reference point of time, and God as the aim of God's creatures (out of grace), then we are not merely talking about a distant ideal for which we vaguely hope and which has no basis in historical reality; something that is still preliminary and immeasurably far away; something that is only a future conceived in the mind.

Instead, we say Easter, resurrection. And that means that the start has been made and the ultimate future has already begun. The transfiguration of the world is not an ideal or a postulate; it is reality. Natural history, with all its developments and evolutions, has reached—in a preliminary fashion, at least—its unsurpassable high point: as material reality, it is also a completely transfigured reality of the glorious body of God in eternity. The most incredible and ultimate evolution of the material world has already happened, naturally so, through the gracious power of God. This evolution has leaped ahead and forward into the eternity of the spirit of God and while doing so was not destroyed by the incomprehensible burning heat of God, but survived and was transformed.

If we really thought about it, we Christians would have to say that we, not the others, are the most radical materialists, because we say that the pure, actual self-communication of God, or God's divine word, has taken on forever a true body. Human history has already reached in one of its representatives—or rather, in *the* representative—its own end. (We refer only to human history when celebrating Easter, though in Christ and through him the entire history of creation is affected.) This end is not only spirit or transfigured soul, but the entire person who lived out his own history, suffered it, and finished it without any of it being lost, so that everything is now revealed as meaningful and glorious. This end, which is the beginning of the fulfillment of everything, has already come to pass, and it has revealed itself to a humanity that is still moving along in history. It is like a marching throng of people, where the ones at the head have already arrived at their destination and are joyously waving to those who are still marching in back, shouting: We have arrived, the goal has been found, it is just as we had hoped.

The place where this beginning was made and the destination that was reached is called Jesus of Nazareth, the crucified and risen one. Because his tomb was empty and he, the dead one, has proved to be the living one in the totality of his concrete humanity, we know: Everything has already begun to be well. Just about everything is still in the process of moving, yet it is a movement to an end that is not utopia but imminent reality.

People like to give half answers. They like to take refuge in what requires no definite decision. That is understandable: We are moving, hence are in a state in which everything, such as meaning and meaninglessness, death and life, is still jumbled, unfinished, and half-way. But it cannot remain this way. Things are progressing. And the end can be nothing other than full concreteness. Therefore, reality demands of us a clear answer given with our life, whether we like it or not. The question we are asked is: death or life, meaning or meaninglessness? We are asked to choose between ideals that are nebulous and non-committal on the one hand and concrete facts on the other. If we decide for meaning and for life by faith and action (assuming that the terms "life" and "death" are not concrete enough for our taste); if we accept life and meaning completely and in their immeasurable magnitude and breath, not just partially, then we have said "yes" to Easter, whether we know it or not.

We Christians know that the reality of Easter is not just the secret essence of our existence, but is the explicitly named and known truth and reality of our faith. And, therefore, we can say the words of Easter that capture the entire history of nature and the world in a celebration at whose center stands the one who is being celebrated, thereby pronouncing for everything that this history contains the final word: I believe in the resurrection of the dead and in life everlasting. I believe that the beginning of the glory of everything that exists has already begun to unfold, that we, who appear to be doomed and lost, searching and wandering, are already enveloped into infinite blessedness. For the end has already had its beginning. And it is glorious.

A FAITH THAT LOVES THE EARTH

It is difficult to express in worn human words the mystery contained in the joy of Easter. If the mysteries of the gospel can enter the smallness of our human comprehension only with great difficulty, putting them into human words involves even greater difficulty. The Easter message is the most human message of Christianity. It is the reason we have such a hard time understanding it. For what is the most true and obvious, in short, the easiest, is also the hardest to live out, to do, and to believe. This is the case today because we have accepted the silent and hence undisputed assumption that religion is solely about a deep feeling of the heart and an advanced spiritual life, which we have to attain by ourselves and which, as a result, suggests that the thoughts and sentiments of the heart stand in stark contrast to reality.

But Easter says: God has done something. He has. And his deed has not simply touched the heart of this or that person in some subtle way, so that it now trembles a little before the unspeakable and the unnamable one. God has raised his son from death. God has made what was dead alive. God has conquered death. God has done something and declared victory in a place that has nothing to do with one's interiority, in a place that despite all the praiseworthiness of reason makes us most ourselves, in a place of earthly reality, far away from all mere thought and spiritual disposition, namely, where we experience *what* we are: children of the earth who have to die.

We are children of this earth. Birth and death, body and earth, bread and wine are our life; and the earth is our homeland. In the midst of all that, of course, there is a secret essence of spirit, of subtle, tender, seeing spirit who looks toward eternity, and the soul, which infuses everything with life and lightness. But the spirit, or the soul, has to be present, has to be where we are, on this earth and in the body, clothing them with its eternal gleam instead of acting like a pilgrim who, ghostlike, wanders across the stage of the world once while remaining misunderstood and out of place there. We are too much children of the earth to be able to leave the earth behind completely. And if heaven is to help us make life on earth bearable, then it will have to bend low and appear as a blessed light above this earth and break forth as a gleam from the earth's dark center.

We are of the earth. We can become disloyal to it because of our stubbornness or self-aggrandizement, which would not be proper for the children of this humble, serious Mother Earth; or we can be loyal because, after all, we have to be who we are, meaning that we are united with earth's secret pain, which we feel deep inside our own being. The earth, our great mother, is also concerned. She suffers from her impermanent nature. Her most joyous feasts can suddenly become like the start of a funeral, and when one hears her laughing, one is afraid that beneath the laughter weeping will suddenly arise. She brings forth children who die, who are too weak to live forever and have too much spirit to do without eternal joy, because they can, in contrast to the animals of the earth, see the end even before it has come and are not mercifully spared the conscious experience of this end. The earth births children of immense appetites, and what she gives them is too beautiful to be ignored by them and too little to ever satisfy them. And since the earth is the place of this unhappy incongruence between the great promise that keeps on calling and the meager gift that does not satisfy, she also becomes the vast field of her children's guilt, so that they try to rip from her more than she is able to give. She may argue that she has become this way only through the original guilt of the first person on earth, Adam. But it makes no difference: She is the unhappy mother now, too alive and too beautiful to be able to send her children away from her so they might acquire for themselves a new home of eternal life and too poor to fully meet their longing, a longing she herself has bequeathed to them. Most of the time, she manages neither one nor the other, since she is always both life and death, and the muddy mixture she hands her children in the form of life and death, rejoicing and mourning, creative deed and repetitive labor is called our everyday life. Thus, we are here on earth, our permanent home, and yet that is not enough. And the adventure of leaving this earthly home is impossible not because of our cowardice but rather on account of our loyalty to who we are.

What should we do then? We should hear the message of the resurrection of the Lord! Is Christ the Lord risen from the dead or not? We believe in his resurrection, hence we confess: He died, he descended to the dead, and the third day he rose again. But what does that mean and why is this message a blessing to the children of the earth?

He who is both the son of God and a human being has died. The one who has died is both the eternal fullness of divinity, which is sovereign, unlimited, and blessed as the word of the Father before all time *and* the child of the earth as son of the blessed mother. The one who has died is, therefore, both the son of God's perfected nature and the child of earth's poverty. But to have died does not mean (as we might think along the lines of non-Christian spiritualism) that his spirit or his soul, the receptacle of his eternal divinity, has escaped from this world and this earth and has fled to the distant land of God's glory beyond. It cannot mean this simply because the body that is related to the earth was broken by death and because the murderous earth has demonstrated that a child of eternal light cannot be housed in earth's darkness.

We may say that he died, but we need to add immediately that he also descended to the dead and rose. We need to add this in order free his death from overtones of fleeing the world, overtones that we are inclined to add. Jesus himself said that he would descend into the heart of the earth (Mt 12:40), namely to the heart of all earthly things, where everything is interconnected and one, to the seat of death and earth's impermanence. This is where he proceeded to go in death. By the holy strategy of his eternal nature, he allowed himself to be conquered by death so as to be swallowed up by it and to thereby reach earth's very center, where he could, amidst all that gives birth and forms the world's common root, infuse it forever with his divine life. Especially because he died, he belongs to the earth, for putting someone's body into earth's grave means that the person (or the soul, as we would say) who has died enters not only into relationship with God but also into that final union with the mysterious ground of being, where all space-time elements are tied together and have their point of origin. In his death, the Lord descended into the lowest and deepest region of what is visible. It is no longer a place of impermanence and death, because there *he* now is. By his own death, he has become the heart of this earthly world, God's heart in the center of the world, where the world even before its own unfolding in space and time taps into God's power and might.

And he rose from this heart of all earthly things where ultimate union and utter nothingness could no longer be distinguished and from which emanates the entire course of the world. He rose, not in order to go away in the end, not so that the pains of death could give birth to him anew, leaving the earth's dark womb in hopelessness and void. No, he is risen in his body. That means: He has begun to transfigure this world into himself; he has accepted this world forever; he has been born anew as a child of the earth, but of an earth that is transfigured, freed, unlimited, an earth that in him will last forever and is delivered from death and impermanence for good. He is risen to show not that he is leaving the tomb of the earth forever, but that this very tomb of the dead—which is the body and the earth—has been completely transformed into the glorious, incomprehensible home of the living God and the divine soul of the son. By rising, he has not left the dwelling of the earth, since he still has his body, though in a final and transfigured way, and is a part of the earth, a part that still belongs to the earth and is connected to earth's nature and destiny. He is risen in order to reveal that by his death there remains forever implanted into earth's narrowness and pain, within her heart, the life of freedom and blessedness.

What we mean by Jesus' resurrection and thoughtlessly consider his private fate is, in fact, in terms of the totality of what is real, the first indication that behind this so-called experience of an event (which we consider so important), the true and decisive nature of things has actually changed. His resurrection is like the first erupting of a volcano, which shows that the fire of God is already burning inside the world and its light will eventually bring everything else to a blessed glow. He is risen to show that it has already started. The new forces of a transfigured world are already at work at the heart of the same world that forced him there in death; new forces are conquering impermanence, sin, and death at their core; and it will take only a little time in history, which we call *post Christum natum*, until everywhere—not just in the body of Jesus—what has happened will become visible . Because he did not begin to heal, save, and transfigure the world on the level of surface appearances but at its innermost root, we creatures living on the world's surface think that nothing has happened. Because the waters of suffering and of guilt are flowing where *we* are, we assume that they have not yet been stopped deep down at their source. Because malice is still carving big letters onto the face of the earth, we conclude that love has died at the deepest core of nature. But all of that is illusion. And we consider that illusion to be life's reality.

He is risen because by death he has conquered and delivered earthly existence at its very core. And, in rising, he has retained this core. And so he has remained. When we confess him as risen to God in heaven, we are saying that he is withdrawing from us his concrete transfigured humanity for a little while, and we are saying, moreover, that there is no longer a chasm between God and the world. Christ is already at the very heart of all the lowly things of the earth that we are unable to let go of and that belong to the earth as mother. He is at the heart of the nameless yearning of all creatures, waiting—though per-

haps unaware that they are waiting—to be allowed to participate in the transfiguration of his body. He is at the heart of
earth's history, whose blind progress amidst all victories and all
defeats is headed with uncanny precision toward the day that
is his, where his glory will break forth from its own depths,
thereby transforming everything. He is at the heart of all tears
and all death as concealed rejoicing and as the life that gains
victory by its apparent death. He is at the heart of one's hand-
ing something to a beggar as the secret wealth that is bestowed
on the giver. He is at the heart of the miserable defeats of his
servants as the victory that is God's. He is at the heart of our
weakness as the power that is allowed to appear weak because
it is invincible. He is even at the heart of sin as the patient
mercy of everlasting love that remains until the end. As the
most secret law and the innermost nature of all things, he is
what still triumphs and prevails when all other laws appear to
be dissolving. He is with us like the light of the day and the air
to which we pay no attention, like the secret law of a movement, a law that we do not grasp because the duration of the
movement that we *can* experience is too short to allow us to
detect its underlying formula. But he is here, the heart of this
earthly world and the secret seal of its everlasting promise.

Therefore, we children of the earth may love the earth,
should love her, even where she is terrifying and tormenting us
with her poverty and death-dealing impermanence. Since he
has entered her forever through death and resurrection, her
misery has become what is only preliminary and serves merely
as a test for our faith in earth's innermost secret—the risen
one. That this is the hidden meaning of earth's poverty is generally not our experience...but our faith can blessedly defy
experience. It is a faith that can love the earth since she is, or
will become, the body of the risen one. Therefore, we do not
have to depart from her, for God's life dwells in her. If we are
looking for the God of eternity (and how could we not be?)
and for an earth that is accommodating as she is and meant
to serve as our eternal chosen home, then this is the *one* way

to find *both*, for in the resurrection of the Lord, God has shown that he has adopted the earth forever.

In a play of words that is hard to translate, an ancient father of the church once said: *Caro cardo salutis*, the flesh is the connecting point of salvation. The place that is safe from all the pain of sin and death is not the beyond, but lies in the one who descended and lives in the innermost nature of our flesh. The most sophisticated religion aiming at escape from the world could never bring down from the distant heights of eternity the God of our life and of earth's salvation, and neither could it go to him in the beyond. But he himself has come to us. And he has transformed what we are and what we should always regard as the faint earthly remainder of our spiritual existence: the flesh. Since that time, Mother Earth has brought forth only children that will be transfigured, for his resurrection is the beginning of the resurrection of all flesh.

One thing is necessary, though, for this irreversible deed of his to become the blessing of our life. He also has to burst open the grave of our heart, to rise from the center of our being where he is the power and the promise. There he is still in the process of doing this. There it is still Holy Saturday until the last day, which will be the day of Easter for the entire cosmos. Such a resurrection happens in the freedom of our faith. Even there it is *his* deed. But it is his deed occurring as ours: as a loving faith that allows us to be brought along on this unimaginable journey of all earthly reality headed toward its own glory, a journey that started with the resurrection of Christ.

MYSTICISM OF THE EARTH
John 2:1–12

In telling of the Lord, the gospel writer John always sees in the midst of the everyday that which is eternal, earthly events as mirroring heavenly ones.

There is a wedding. People drink and laugh. The waiters rush back and forth and the wine is good. The atmosphere is congenial and everyone seems happy to contribute freely to the joyous mood while drinking wine. The quiet woman from Nazareth, who could not have easily been omitted from the list of invited guests, is actually no problem, though one was a little afraid of that. She is even concerned with keeping the festivities in full swing. She recognizes a potential problem before others do. How human are the true children of heaven!

The son of this woman is also there, along with his friends, for the more guests, the more fun the celebration. He, too, like his mother, appears somewhat mysterious. But, strangely enough, he settles into the circumstances, even though things are rather casual today. No, he is no spoil-sport. Who would have thought that of him? One was a little afraid that he might launch into deep sermons. But no. Where earthly joy threatens to run out along with the wine, he performs his first miracle. He does this quietly and unobtrusively, so that even a miracle of God will not disturb human festivities.

He loves humans, he who himself is human. He loves people, their earth and their joy, the taste of wine, and the carefree laughter of a childlike heart. (Later, those who cannot stand themselves will call him a glutton and a drunkard.) This is the start of his signs. He will bring this start to its fulfillment and completion. He will soak the earth with his blood in the concreteness of the cross and under the sign of wine. He will transform the waters of bitterness into the wine of everlasting joy. He will preserve the earth, the body of the human being. It will be transfigured, not done away with. When in the end the glory of his divinity breaks through, the earth—the body—will not perish in the light of this burning glory but will be affirmed by it. Forever and ever!

He did not come to lead the spirits from the dark dungeon that holds them captive; he came to redeem the flesh to its full, transfigured nature. The reason that the Son of Man goes to the wedding is because the flesh is trying to dominate again.

He takes the cup, fills it with the wine of the earth, drinks it, and offers it to all of these young people who do not know what is happening. It will still take a long time until this earth and its people are redeemed. It will cost his tears and his blood until this earth is cleansed and until people dare to believe that they can be human forever without becoming animals or angels. It will cost his blood until people understand and are able to love this earth and God: God, because without him the earth is nothing, the earth, because it is the sacrament of God. He performs the miracle with the wine of the earth to propose a childlike, joyous earthly existence. His eyes are looking ahead and his heart longs for the day when he will once again and forever drink of the fruit of the vine at the wedding feast of the lamb in the kingdom of God, together with all those his Father has blessed, for the day when there will be not only a new heaven but also a new earth.

CORPUS CHRISTI AND PENTECOST

FEAST OF DAILY BREAD

The feast of Corpus Christi is a strange feast. It lifts up what is daily celebrated in our churches in quiet simplicity: the mystery of the altars. It displays in festive procession what each day is not only displayed but also received, the holy bread of eternal life. It lifts high in a conspicuous manner what is eaten, namely the heavenly manna. It is almost as if the feast tries to make a celebration out of what happens each day and yet fails at it because everyday life can celebrate much better what really matters than one feast day by itself: that we are receiving this bread of eternal life as pilgrims who are traveling between time and eternity, are receiving it daily, until the journey ends and an unveiled God becomes our eternal bread of glory. Regardless, we celebrate this feast so as not to completely forget what we celebrate each day: the meal of pilgrims who are en route to eternal life.

How much we need this meal! As pilgrims we are still on the way, unsteadily moving through the preliminary. The fact that we are walking among shadows and analogies in faith's darkness is our inevitable fate and a beneficial burden, and neither should surprise us much. What is highest is also the farthest away and remains the promised prize of a freely exercised faithfulness in the midst of the preliminary. But we would like to have this highest already, even though and especially since we are walking so as to find it. How else could we be on this pilgrimage unless we knew that the strength of eternity was within, and how else could we hope unless the hoped-for were already near? God can be sought only with the help of God, and we would not be seeking God had we not always known him to be found and had he not allowed us to find him daily. Hence, both must be true: promise and prize, path and destination are here already, and so is God, who is with us yet still hidden beneath the veil of his own creatures.

If, then, the blessed meal of eternity is offered to us here in the temporal world, the nature of that meal matches the sober modesty of a pilgrim people: simple and ordinary, hidden beneath the earthly signs of everyday existence where there already lies what one believes must be clung to with expectation and love. And so the Lord has prepared a meal: offering to the senses a sign, revealing himself in the form of a little bread and wine that ordinarily sustain our body and make the spirit rejoice. Wherever this meal is celebrated at his command and by his authority, wherever one celebrates the remembrance of his last meal in his words and thereby truly moves the meal into the present, there he is present in flesh and body as the inner truth and reality of these concrete signs, and there he becomes the bread of unending strength and the wine of unspeakable joy. He himself allows his body to become for us in the present moment the sign of what he wishes to be for us in his spirit, the God who has given his own life to the poor creature. And only as we receive the bread of the altars, he becomes for us what he is: the earthly one by which God's eternity enters our small and narrow mortal existence. The human head bows over what looks like a common piece of bread and, in fact, bears only a faint resemblance to actual bread; the human hand reaches for the cup that commonly holds only the beverage of this earthly life. But then there occurs what is the innermost aim of all happenings: God and the believing heart, respectively, breaking through all possible barriers in order to meet in the one who is both, in whom the union has already been made man-

ifest ultimately and bodily, in the Lord, that is, who is both
the eternal word from above and the son of the earth, born of
a virgin. He holds the body of this earth, the painfully born
and sacrificed; we fall again into the depth of his own fate,
suffered so long ago, when we take what he has taken from us,
and we remain where we and he also has remained, directly
with God. O holy meal, in which Christ can be enjoyed, the
memory of his passion renewed, the soul filled with grace, and
the pledge of the coming glory obtained!

In our own everyday experience we regard as ordinary the
mystery of eternal life offered to a dying world. See how the
priest routinely administers it, driven by duty's call as if
merely carrying out a secular duty and not celebrating the
liturgy where heavenly light and blessedness intertwine! See
the narrow and parched hearts into which the Lord descends
and which, at their best, have nothing else to report to him
but a few self-absorbed wishes of theirs that make up their
daily life! Oh, we Christians! We receive both the pure
blessedness of heaven and the delicate, transfigured essence of
earth's bittersweet fruit in this sacrament, receiving as ultimate truth what is encapsulated in the hard shell of the everyday. And we receive it as if nothing had happened; tired and
weary we carry home from God's table our old hearts into the
narrow rooms of our lives, where we are more comfortable
than in the high-ceilinged hall of God. We sacrifice the son
and want to preserve ourselves; we participate in the divine
liturgy and are not seriously engaged. Perhaps we bring our
good will, but it has little power over the dulled sluggishness
of our hearts. And yet, perhaps this, too, is part of the sign
that even at this point God is already moving toward his creatures and the meal of eternal life is already being celebrated
when still short of its fulfillment. When the meal of eternal
life is being prepared within the narrow confines of time, it is
not surprising that those who come to it are poor and their
small minds and cramped hearts do not yet comprehend what
they receive.

It is understandable, then, that we should feel a little troubled and taxed, almost forced into nervous embarrassment before such divine excess. It is through grace, his grace bestowed on us, that we come nonetheless, that we partake of the meal at his table—as long as we come, as long as we drag ourselves to him, we who are sad and bent over, strained and burdened. He welcomes us, even though we lack the joyous gleam in our eyes at his presence. But he who has descended into the inner depths of the earth can bear this too and is not hurt when he, upon entering the dull narrowness of our hearts, finds there only a small glimmer of love and good will. With the same patience that God has with our weakness, the greatest sacrament wants to be the sacrament of our everyday life.

It is proper for us to celebrate at least once a year the feast of that feast which we celebrate daily, since we have come to participate in it from such a long distance and because we make of the daily feast a ritual of such labor and strain. It is an annual feast that says that the ordinary is the most extraordinary, the daily participation in it is the content of eternity, the small earthly bread is God's arrival among us and the start of the transfiguration of all earthly reality. Therefore, let us celebrate today a feast that is a mixture of consolation and sadness—a sadness over the fact that we are celebrating daily the mystery of our Lord in non-festive ways, a consolation that he is with us every day until the end, regardless. It is a feast in which the past becomes present by our remembrance of the Lord's Supper and where by his death all distance of time is overcome; and it is a feast in which the future becomes present because beneath the sacrament's veil lies what the future will bring, namely the God of eternal love who is already near. Each day God prepares for us his feast, the holy meal. Today, on the feast of Corpus Christi, we ourselves should prepare a meal for God out of our deep gratitude that he prepares one for us daily, where pilgrims may receive strength and joy in order to find their way home, along their earthly paths, to the meal of eternal life.

WALK WITH THE LORD

Today the church carries its sacrament in festive procession through all places of human life. Amidst the joyous singing of hymns, the church walks through the streets of the world and shows the world in an almost frightening exuberance of rejoicing her most intimate secret, namely, the blessed presence of her Lord. In this celebratory activity of walking and singing, the church is seemingly quite oblivious as to whether we ourselves are in a festive and joyous mood, whether we can really bring ourselves to do what we are asked to do on this feast. Each year, on a set day, the church dares to have a procession that can be truly celebrated only when one is cheerful, relaxed, and free of life's burdens. That in itself is reason for concern: Can I join in the celebration or is my heart too heavy?

When one hears the rejoicing and sees the festive, blessed display and considers what exactly it is that is being displayed, there is another concern that might make the heart almost skip a beat. Not that one would disparage this festive celebration. God forbid. Where else should people celebrate if not here in the streets, where it is quite evident that we are fallen sinners, empty and bound, yet saved unto freedom for God's holy majesty? What causes concern about the singing and celebrating is the fact that what is being celebrated here is death. For it is written: As often as you do this, you are proclaiming the death of our Lord until he comes. The Lord instituted this sacrament the night when he was betrayed to death. He said: Do this in remembrance of me, so that we would ever remember by this celebration the sacrifice in which his body was broken, his blood was shed, and his forsaken soul was surrendered into the hands of an incomprehensible God. Truly that is how it is: The heart could skip a beat when rejoicing under a blue sky amidst the aromas of flowers and incense because we are carrying beneath the arcades of blessed song the sign of someone who has died, and not just anyone, but the word of God who has become flesh. How incomprehensible it makes human beings and their existence seem when an event in which the utter gloom of falling into the deepest bottomless abyss can become a celebration of childlike, innocent joy. We proclaim the death of our Lord until he comes. Let us not forget that today. We remember this death not as the death of joy but as the bottomless abyss from which springs forth mysteriously, as from a never-ceasing fountain, the true joy of this day.

Look at these people in procession. Dressed in festive garb, they are singing and walking in a way that is reminiscent of King David dancing before the ark of the covenant. Where are they going? If one has the courage to ask and the courage to answer seriously while carefully considering every angle, can one then really skip one answer, even if it is only a part of the whole: They are going into their death? Wherever one walks, there is instability. Wherever there is time, there is already death, the end of temporal movement. Hence, when those who are walking in their festive garb are done doing so, they have walked closer to death, their own death, which mercilessly has moved closer to them in a few hours, and to the same degree as if they had spent the time bitterly crying. And after this festive walk, things don't stop; they continue. But this and that walk, these stony paths and those broad streets are equally steps along the same path. And this path goes to where it ends, where everything that walks and moves comes to its final, single end.

It is strange: Those walking today, those who have decorated the external street of their internal walk toward death, are carrying along on their serious walk through festive streets the one who has died like they have to die, who has died for those who have to die, who has died for them because they have to die. That is the one they have with them on their walk. They carry along into their own death the one who was killed. Why would they do that? Do they not press death close to their own hearts when carrying this body, while hoping that by moving they can delay the end? Why a procession of the

blessed body, of the one who was killed, a procession marked
by songs, rather than tears of hopeless despair? They do this
precisely because he has died; because it is the son of God and
life itself that has died; because they have with them the one
who has shared their destiny, the one who is God and not subject to destiny; because he is the one who gave his life of his
own accord and no one could tear it away from him; because
he is the one who conquered death by his own death; because
he is the one who descended into the deepest emptiness in
order to fill it with life eternal.

It is because they have him with them on the Via Dolorosa
of their life that they are allowed to laugh and to sing and walk
their serious path in this procession. They are also allowed to
cry. They may walk along just as they are, dusty from the
streets of life, a little tired and worn, disposed to neither
laughter nor tears, living right between the lowest lows and
the most blessed highs of existence, walking a street that may
be either the Via Triumphalis or the Via Dolorosa. They may
do anything, be anything when walking, as long as they are
part of the walk. After all, he is the one who has already cried
the tears of their death, who has descended into death's deepest abyss, to the place where no one else has gone. As he goes
along with them, now in the sacrament and at all other times
in daily life by the grace of his spirit, those processing are
praying and saying about him: suffered under Pontius Pilate,
dead and buried, he descended into hell. But they are also
praying and saying about him that he is the eternal word of the
Father, wisdom, light, and power, life and the resurrection.
When the sign of his most cruel death is blessedly raised above
those who kneel, it means: Under the sign of death that blesses
those on their path toward it, life is present and not death, the
life that transformed death into life's own victory. And therefore the street of our life becomes once a year for us Christians
a Via Triumphalis; therefore, we follow after the one who by
carrying life itself has become our life when sharing our death.
He walks ahead of us. His sacrament proclaims his death and

also ours. Since he goes ahead of us, he does not cover up the truth with dulling, harmless niceties, but says: You share my fate that you proclaim with this sacrament; you share its hardness, its difficulty, and its relentlessness. And we say by this holy procession: Your fate is also ours in its entirety of which is written: I was dead, but see, I am alive forever; and I have the keys of death and of Hades (Rev 1:18).

We cannot fully grasp the enormity of what such a procession means in connection with the one who died and lives. Who could comprehend God and world, life and death, time and eternity as the unity that this celebration entails? All we can do is walk, ever being led through new realities, of which this present procession is only a sign. It is true that one day our path is blessed and a wide street opens up to distant goals, the next day it is a path of sorrows. One day it is a dusty path in the open fields amidst barren lands, the next day a dead-end street. About them all, scripture says: People are not the masters of their paths. But all paths should be leading to the one path, the one that leads to God, or, as the psalms often say: All ways, regardless of whether they include joy or death, should aim at the one goal. All paths should lead toward the vast fullness of God, where paths no longer exist because one has arrived, has reached a pathless fullness and a true home.

When looking at the sacramental path of today's procession, we do not want to forget the other paths for which the present one is only a sign, an acknowledgment, and a promise. And so we want to remember them also: the paths of our own lives, the paths of those who walk them with great difficulty and are poor and burdened, perhaps without knowing the secret destination of their seemingly erroneous or aimless pilgrimage; the path of those who are ruled by the enemies of Christianity, those who are not allowed to participate in such glad processions and have to walk, in faith, the way of the cross on the heels of the one who carries it. We also want to pray that God may give us the grace of a small procession at the end of our life, even if it consists only of the quiet prayer of a priest in street clothes as we make our last turn on the journey of this life, a prayer that may be our nourishment for the path to life eternal, where our path ends, so that through the sacrament, or at least by its grace, the Lord may accompany us on our last steps and we be led from the path of this dying life, in Christian discipleship, to the blessed path of life eternal and God's inexpressible glory.

PRAYER FOR PENTECOST

Lord Jesus Christ, son of the Father, sacrament of life, bread of pilgrims, food for the journey and its aim, path, and home, be adored, loved, and praised in your sacrament.

Lord, today is Pentecost. Today we celebrate the day on which you, raised above the highest heavens and seated at the right hand of the Father, poured out the spirit of promise upon us, so that you would remain by your spirit with us all the days until the end and so that by it you might continue in us your life and death for the glory of the Father and for our salvation.

Lord, look at the spirits that press upon us and grant us the spiritual gift of discernment. What a fitting gift for Pentecost this would be!

Grant us the understanding, validated by daily life, that by looking at and longing for you, we may experience your spirit emerging as the spirit of calm, of peace and confidence, of freedom and simple clarity, while all unrest and fear, narrowness and leaden pride are recognized as at most our own spirit or the one of the deep dark.

Grant us the spirit of your consolation. Lord, we are aware that even in times of desolation, dearth, and spiritual powerlessness, we are called to be, have to be, and are able to be faithful. Yet, we still are permitted to ask you for the spirit of consolation and strength, of joy and confidence, of growth in faith, hope, and love, of noble service and praise of your

Father, for the spirit of quiet and peace. From our hearts drive out spiritual desolation, darkness, confusion, inclination toward what is low and earthly, distrust, hopelessness, lukewarmness, sadness, the sense of loneliness, ambiguity, and the strangling notions that would lead us away from you.

If it should please you to guide us there, however, then leave with us during such hours and days, we pray, at least the Holy Spirit of fidelity, steadfastness, and perseverance, so we can in sure trust continue our path, maintain its direction, remain true to the principles chosen back then when your light shone upon us and your joy made our heart glad. At those times when we feel deserted like that, grant us then especially your spirit of courageous attack, of firm prayer of defiance, of self-discipline, of penance. Grant us then the unshakable confidence that even during times of feeling deserted we are not deserted by your grace, that you are with us even more so when we cannot see you as the strength that wants to be victorious in our weakness. Grant us the spirit of truly remembering your kind visitations in the past and of being on the lookout for the concrete evidence of your love, evidence that is bound to come. During such hours of desolation, allow us to confess our sinfulness and poverty, to humbly experience our weakness, and to acknowledge that you alone are the sure source of all good and all heavenly consolation.

When your consolation comes, grant that it may be accompanied by the spirit of humility and readiness to serve you even during times without consolation.

Grant us always the spirit of courage and the steadfast resolve to acknowledge scruples and temptation, not to argue with temptation, not to compromise with it, but to say a definite "no" because it is the simplest strategy for winning in battle. Grant us the humility to ask for advice in dark times, without talkativeness and navel-gazing, but also without the foolish pride that says we should always be able to manage on our own. Grant us the spirit of heavenly wisdom, so that we can realize the true place of danger in our character and in our life, to be most faithfully on the alert there and to fight where we are most vulnerable.

In other words, grant us your spirit of Pentecost, the fruits of the spirit, which are, in the apostle's words, love, joy, peace, patience, mildness, mercy, trust, gentleness, humility, self-discipline. If we have this spirit and its fruits, we are no longer slaves to the law but free children of God. Then the spirit within us says: Abba, dear Father. Then it intercedes for us in groans too deep for words, then it is balm, seal, and pledge of life eternal. Then it is the source of the living waters that spring up in the heart and rise to eternal life, whispering: Let us go home to the Father!

O Jesus, send us your spirit. Grant your Pentecost gift more and more. Make clear our spiritual eye and enlarge our spiritual capacity to be sensitive, so that we can distinguish your spirit from all the others. Grant us your spirit, so it may be said of us: If the spirit of the one who raised Jesus from the dead lives in you, it will also raise your mortal body to life eternal through the spirit dwelling in you.

It is Pentecost, Lord. Your men and women servants are praying that you make them capable of the boldness that you ask of them. Let it be Pentecost in us also, now and forevermore. Amen.

LOVE FOR GOD AND NEIGHBOR

THE FIRST COMMANDMENT
Matthew 22:34–40

These days, much is being discussed and written about loving our neighbor. Non-Christians engage in speaking and writing on this topic by borrowing the message from Christianity, since they don't have it in their own heritage. And Christians do it because, since not much loving of neighbor is actually being done, one likes to at least make mention of it. Both discussing and writing are good, for it is necessary to repeatedly preach on this subject, to exhort, admonish, and warn. One cannot talk enough about loving one's neighbor, provided, of course, that one does not just talk about it to avoid practicing it. Still, one should not forget what is written in today's gospel: the first commandment is to love God, to love God with one's whole heart, one's whole soul, one's whole mind. This love cannot be replaced by leading a "proper life," or by loving one's neighbor, or by philanthropy, or by social justice. Of course, these too are necessary. But they don't constitute a love for God. And that is precisely what is expected of us: the great, the living and heartfelt love, which is such an important and unique commandment that one needs to forget that it is a commandment so as to love not in response to a requirement but because God is God.

This strange commandment does not ask of us a performance, an action that can be measured and, when completed, puts us in a position of saying that we have met our obligation. The type of love required demands our own heart, the deepest and the most ultimate, which is ourselves. We would rather give everything else than ourselves. Everything can be measured and obligations can be met, but one cannot do that with the heart. The heart will have to give itself completely to God, forever and not by degrees. Do we love God like that? Do we love God as the one who loves, the one who is near and faithful, the one who asks for our heart by offering us his own eternal one? Or is God for us only the name of the highest, yet rather impersonal imaginary world regime that one respects, that one should not get into conflict with, that one tends to avoid by obeying its commandments? It is almost easier to fear God than to truly love God. And yet, it is precisely this love that is called for, so much so that all fear of God (if only we truly had it!) would not avail us much without this love. For condemnation is ultimately only our desperate inability to love God.

Our heart is so sluggish and tired. It is used up by everyday life. And God is so far away. That is how it appears to the spiritually blind and lame. That is why our heart thinks it cannot love. When love is preached, the heart remains mute, unmoved, and stubborn, and even one's own "good will" is insufficient to command the heart to love. No, we do not have such love as is spoken of in the first commandment. Only the one who is asking for such love from us can give it to us. So, let us at least ask him for it. We need to pray for this love, for God himself has to pour it out into our hearts through the Holy Spirit. God has to give the life, the light, and the power of such love. God has to be able to love himself in us and through us by his Holy Spirit in order for our love to be adequate.

Humble fright about our lack of love with regard to God is the grace-induced beginning of our love. The prayer for the love of God, a prayer that protests against the heart's secret and concealed dislike of God, is our beginning of loving God, and we can make such a beginning because God continually offers us his grace. In worship, we often recite a prayer to awaken the so-called three divine virtues. One would hope that we are especially asking for love that only God can give, even though he calls for it in the commandment that will ever be the first. God will answer such a prayer. For God promises it in his own word. And we should believe him more than our own heart. When it is praying for love, then it loves, even if it is not aware of more than the pain of knowing that it has, up until now, only very poorly fulfilled the first of the commandments.

THE NEW COMMISSION OF THE ONE LOVE

The topic [we are discussing here] is the unity of love of neighbor and love of God. Are these simply two things that stand next to each other, loosely connected through a commandment from God, so that one can only properly love God when the commandment of loving one's neighbor is equally respected and carried out to the best of one's ability? Or is there a closer relationship between the two?

One could assume that God has commanded all kinds of things and that obeying these various commandments is only a test and the concrete fulfillment of what he wants ultimately, namely that people love *him*, the eternal God, from their very core and with their entire heart and with all their strength. But that is actually not true. The love of God and the love of neighbor are in much closer relationship than is commonly assumed. And so, we want to reflect on that a little.

In addition to the importance of the subject matter itself, there is a critical point that relates to today's situation. We Christians would be wrong to ignore this point, namely, that contemporary people have a hard time with the question of God. The world seems to be closed up, so to speak. To have a relationship with God—the living, otherworldly, eternal one—is not as easy for people today as it was in earlier days, when one had the possibly justified idea that one could positively identify the mysterious workings of God in the world.

People today live in a secular world. We need not reflect here on the dangers this poses and the degree to which this development also has its positive side. A secularized world is the fate of today's Christian, and its causes, extent, and limitations should be anticipated and regarded as a welcome opportunity for examining one's own relationship with God and for reflecting on what it means to be a Christian.

In summary, this is what is true for our current situation, which means that only where people have a genuine, loving, heartfelt relationship with others can they find God and convince others that this reality that we call God exists. All mere theoretical talk, ritualistic activity, or explicitly religious display no longer has any credibility with people today unless it is carried, framed, and corroborated by true love, a love between one human being and another. People today have an almost radical need to demythologize everything, to tear down all facades, to destroy all taboos, and to ask what it is that remains when all slogans are deleted and all ideologies destroyed. What truly remains is only what can be lived out in the act of loving another, provided this love is real.

Perhaps people of today do not practice such love, though they are aware of being obliged to do so and even are willing to acknowledge this obligation—this love—as the one true thing that remains, that is no mere ideology, that is something about which one does not merely make pious or edifying remarks in gatherings, but that is necessary in life, like business and bread. If we Christians are unaware that this love (which still remains despite all the demythologizing and destruction of taboos) is the essence of Christianity, though hidden as within a seed and as something that has yet to unfold and come to fruition; if we are unaware of this fact, then we are not equipped, in my opinion, to truly understand our Christian faith and to witness to it as something with staying power, as something that always springs up anew. Therefore, it seems to me timely and meaningful to say something about the unity of the love of God and the love of neighbor.

One finds this theme already in scripture, which makes mention of two commandments of which the second is of equal importance to the first: the commandment to love God and to love one's neighbor. Paul says that this love is the crown of perfection. He talks about love of neighbor when saying that whoever does it has fulfilled the law as a whole. And he says that this love is the better path. He warns us to keep in mind that this love and doing acts of mercy, as much as they belong together, are not the same. Even if I gave all my possessions to the poor and allowed my body to be burned, if I did not have love, I would amount to nothing. By that, he does not imply that some inner feeling or a devout disposition is enough. The inner disposition has to be expressed in life through tangible acts of love; otherwise it is all empty talk and we remain a noisy gong and a clanging cymbal. We see repeatedly that Paul makes radically concrete the love of neighbor in very distinct terms and that he calls it the fulfillment of the law, the seal of perfection.

This is not necessarily a given. Rather, it is paradoxical and even seems a bit exaggerated, for it almost looks as if Paul is not thinking about God but is developing here an atheist ethic of Christianity.

Why has the law been fulfilled when I have loved my neighbor? Why is this love not just a piece of the whole but the entire seal of perfection? Why is it that by this love, according to the Lord, the entire law and the prophets are fulfilled? Everything else must have to be contained, then, in this love of neighbor, even and especially the whole, the ultimate, and the crucial: that God be loved. If we disregard John for the moment, scripture tells us that there are not two similar commandments, being of possibly equal importance, being somehow connected, but that one commandment is contained in the other. We can understand that one can love God only by loving one's neighbor. But in Paul, it looks as if one *already* loves God when one loves one's neighbor.

How is this possible? One gains more insight through the first letter of John, which asks how one can love God who is invisible when one does not love one's brother who is visible.

Of course, it is possible to say that this is a simplistic argument that does not say much: if you do not love your neighbor, who is concretely and practically there in your life, how will you be capable of loving the invisible God, who is far away from concrete life experience? It seems, however, that John is actually saying more than that, for in the fourth chapter of this letter one finds the strange statement that says God is in us. And obviously, this is the basis for the possibility of already loving God when loving one's neighbor with true authenticity and wholehearted engagement. To put this in terms of scholastic theology, the thesis is that the love of God and the love of neighbor are mutually dependent, so that when people express themselves in selflessness, in absolute engagement, in true voluntary surrender of self to the other human "you" and are truly doing what love of neighbor entails, then they are already loving God, though they may not know it, though they may not be able to name it, though they may not make explicit mention of this so-called God as the motive of their neighborly love. The thesis aims at saying that when people truly love their neighbor, they drop into and penetrate the ultimate depths of their existence, the ultimate realities of the world and creation and are—without necessarily calling it this—mysteriously encountering the God of their eternal, supernatural salvation by virtue of their love.

How can one support such a thesis? One might begin by looking more closely at scholastic theology, which knows of three theological virtues. This is to say that scholastic theology knows of three ways by which human beings deal with God directly in the depths of their hearts and are guided by the Holy Spirit, by God's spirit, and no longer merely by the realities of the world. In other words, there are three basic ways by which humans are ultimately oriented toward the God of eternal life in his own glory and sovereignty, ways by which we all can become the true, immediate partners of God. The three basic human acts by which people become directly involved with God—the triune God of eternal life—are faith, hope, and love. And, as Paul says, only these three remain.

But theology also says that our neighbor could and should be loved with the divine basic power of love, in which faith and hope are already contained and integrated. If as Christians we really love our neighbor in a salvific way, then this act is not merely the fulfillment of some divine commandment, managed with God's help, but is an ultimate and completely eternal event in life, where we meet God directly.

Whenever we love our neighbor with the supernatural love of God, then and only then do salvation, justification, divine life, and eternity happen. Catholic theology leaves no doubt about the existence of such a divine virtue by which people find the other in the depths of their own being. Once again: this is not a matter of looking at others with a certain benevolent regard because one loves God and shies away from transgressing the commandments of one's beloved God in relation to others. Instead, in a truly supernatural love of neighbor, one expresses God's love by the power of God himself.

Saying this and interpreting Catholic theology in this way seems to mean that we already are where we want to be. But that is not totally correct. Of course, when someone loves another out of faith and from the motive of one's love for God, then such charity, such a divine virtue of godly love, is already made concrete; all of this should be quite clear from what has been said so far. And Catholic theology would agree completely; it has agreed for hundreds of years and still does today, as briefly indicated earlier. But I would like to take this thesis still one step further.

I want to say that when one truly lets go of self and loves the other in absolute self-abandon, one has already encountered the silent, inexplicable mystery of God, and this act, then, is carried out by the type of divine self-communication that we call grace and assumes, in the light of such grace, a salvific and eternal meaning.

Let us look at it from another perspective. We meet many people who are not explicitly Christian and do not want to be. Let us assume that they were to love their neighbor, their

brother or sister, or someone else in ultimate, radical selflessness. What happens there? Is it only something commendable
that still lacks some substantial element, or is there already an
ultimate relationship with God present, a relationship that has
yet to unfold, that should somehow bear God's name, that has
yet to be measured and named in its final, inexpressible, yet
given dimension with regard to God, while already existing?
This is exactly what I mean by saying that wherever people are
truly engaged with their whole being and give themselves
away in an ultimate, true, and radical love for their neighbor,
there exists always and everywhere the love of God, or charity.
This is so not because the nature of such an act would force
one to this conclusion, but because the act allows us to live
under the general will of God's salvation. We live in a world
that is always and everywhere oriented toward the eternal life
of God by the secret grace of God unless we are, through
guilty disbelief, shutting ourselves off from this inner, supernatural, grace-filled dynamic of the world.

The act of loving one's neighbor is not some ethical act,
but actually the basic ethical act of human existence. Understanding means to live with one's self, and freedom means ultimately that the free person takes command of self while aiming toward what is ultimate.

Both of these things can happen only in loving communication with the other, the "you." To people in their nature as
spiritual, personal subjects, the world is primarily a world with
others. We do not live in an environment merely filled with all
types of things. Rather, from the perspective of the subject and
the reality that humans encounter, the world has an inner
structure and is ultimately a communication of love with the
other, the "you." The entire material world we deal with, even
in economic and social matters, for example, is basically only
the material, the prerequisite, the effect of a loving communication with the other "you." In the radical freedom that creates
eternity, people may completely dispose of themselves, and this
self-disposal is ultimately either a loving self-opening toward

the human "you" or an ultimate self-refusal in egotism, which casts people into the condemning, deadly loneliness of being lost. Naturally, this basic act of self-disposal is possible only when people, on their part, are reaching for absolute reality and dealing with God in a non-thematic, non-reflexive way. For we do not start having dealings with God when we call upon God explicitly or when we are giving an explicit name to the mystery that we are ever walking toward and that ultimately offers us spiritual freedom and love. In the act of understanding and especially in the act of freedom, we are always and everywhere implicitly dealing with God. When people act in a loving way toward others as the basic act of their existence, then this basic act results from the general sanctifying and salvific will of God, which exists and works also outside the church, is carried out by God's Holy Spirit, by God's grace, and is at least implicitly, but truly, an act of charity, an act of the love of God.

Naturally, one would have to describe more specifically what love of neighbor is and to demonstrate that this love always borders on the mystery of God, even when it is not intended to do so or specifically aimed at it. When we keep quiet, when we forgive, when we give ourselves fully without expectation of reward and step back from ourselves, then we always reach into an infinity that no longer can be described and is nameless, and we are thereby moving toward the divine mystery that permeates and carries our existence and hence are dealing with God. Something like this always happens in the free, loving act of a truly radical self-opening toward one's neighbor, so that this act is already carried out in the present order of God's salvific will by God's grace, and hence is charity.

Wherever people open themselves up to their neighbor in true personal freedom, they have already done more than merely loved this one neighbor, since the act is borne by God's grace. By loving one's neighbor, one has already loved God. One cannot meet one's neighbor in a loving way unless the dynamic of one's spiritual freedom, borne by God's grace, is already the dynamic of the unspeakable holy mystery that we call God.

This does not mean that human love, as it commonly appears, is the equivalent of the specific believing and hoping love of Christians. It only means that in human love one already carries out divine love. Yet the latter needs a point of reference and should make explicit the aim toward which this love is moving, an aim that should be called upon, named, implored, and worshiped explicitly in faith, hope, and love. Human love, which at its deepest level is already divine love by God's grace, should be an explicit love of the named, the explicitly called upon, the God that is meant by it, and the inner unfolding that is implanted in all love by God's grace. This love is compelled to unfold into the explicitly named Christian love of divine charity. Conversely, it is true also that the explicit divine love for the God who is named, even though one does not see him, is already given in the love of neighbor whom one can see.

It is the case that many people are already saved, justified, and sanctified by God's grace, even though they may not know it; and it is also the case that we as Christians believe, hope, and gratefully acknowledge something that is provided to all people by God's supernatural, free, unconditional grace as being offered and as being potentially accepted, even though many do not see themselves as Christians or believers. Still, in the depth of their nature, people can be Christian, specifically whenever they manage with their whole heart and in complete selflessness to love the neighbor, the one they see. We do not know whether they actually are doing so, just as we ourselves do not know that about ourselves. After all, we are ever those who in our activities and in our lives are trying to love God and neighbor as one. Whether we manage to summon this ultimate strength by the efficacious grace of God or whether all we do is shape only a beautiful façade behind which lies and reigns a deep, unacknowledged egotism will be decided at the great divine tribunal. But at least we have begun to try to love God in deed and truth by trying to love our neighbor. All that we experience—our disappointment, our effort, our turmoil—is ultimately only a way of trying to move away from ourselves to the other and to God.

Doing so is difficult and is the ultimate step and the hardest task of our lives. We can always be deceived about it, but when we have managed to get away from ourselves and to our neighbor in a loving way, we have not done so by our own strength but have moved by God's grace toward God; then God, who loves us in order that we might love our neighbor, as John says, has truly grasped us, has pulled us away from ourselves, and has given us in one piece what our eternity is, the arriving at the "you," in whom we also arrive at God.

We can also look at this from a different angle. Jesus says: "Whatever you have done to one of the least of these, you have done unto me." How often we have heard this expression and used it in our own devout, pious speeches! But let us ask ourselves: Is it really possible for Jesus to say that? Is this not legal speech, saying: I give you credit as if you had done unto me what you have done for one of the least of these people? No, this is not legal speech or moral discourse or a bargaining method, for it is truly the case that we encounter in the other person the word of God made flesh because God himself truly lives in the other. And when we love the other and do not block the dynamic of this love by being guilty of rerouting it back to ourselves, then the divine descent into human flesh happens, so that God is where we are and is looking at us through the other person. The divine descent progresses through us and has the effect that we, on account of God's love, are loving our neighbor and are already loving God by loving our neighbor, since we are not able to summon this kind of love apart from the divine love that carries us and that has manifested itself in our neighbor. The so-called Christian side of neighborly love should be taken seriously in word and deed. Whenever another person meets me, there is Christ present asking: Do you desire to love me, the word of God become flesh? And when I answer "Yes," then he replies: Here I am, in the least of my brothers and sisters.

A theological note may be added for clarity. When we take seriously the Christian incarnation, then the word of God become flesh will be the agency, the gateway, the bridge, God's concreteness for us in the same way as in eternity, when we will see God face to face. The humanity of Jesus is neither a barrier between us and God's transcendent grace, nor is it something that happened once in human history so as to be forgotten thereafter. We will always be dealing with the one God who himself became human. In all of eternity, there is no theology that is not also anthropology.

Is it not true that we Christians have not yet fully understood our Christian faith, that the individual doctrinal statements about our faith, as much as we might confess and accept them, are too far apart from one another, so that we have the impression of living in a vastly complicated world of statements, doctrines, and precepts? In reality, it is simply like this: God has become human, and therefore the love of God is love of people, and vice versa. However, this presupposes that, by allowing the deepest movement of human love to develop to its fullest, we allow it to reach its ultimate, radical aim. Where this happens, everything of Christianity is already there, since there is ultimately only one commandment, in the same way that there is for Christians only one God, namely the one who has become flesh in the eternal word and has dwelt among us and remains, not only yesterday and today, but through all eternity.

We know nothing about God unless we know of the human being, the one whom God has accepted as his own reality and in whom is contained the ultimate mystery, the ultimate essence of human nature. We can make the most essential observation about ourselves only when saying: We are the reality that God has been able to make and has made his very own. Only by saying that, by jumping from anthropology to theology, can we understand what we ourselves are. And therefore, we can understand ourselves only by the act in which we alone can understand its motivation, the act by which we become loving ones, people who have lovingly found the other person, not on specially celebrated occasions but in the crass, ordinary, gray life of the everyday. It is there that we find God, and we are justified in saying that all prayer, all worship, all canon law, the entire institution of the church —all these serve only as a means to help us do one thing: to love God and neighbor, since it is impossible for us to love God unless we love God in our neighbor. Wherever we do so, we have truly fulfilled the law, have wrapped the band of perfection around our entire life, and have walked the path of perfection to which Paul referred. Only by realizing that there exists a truly ultimate union of love of God and love of neighbor do we understand Christianity and its divine simplicity. Of course, one needs to explain the divinely simple. Our entire catechism with its content is the true and authentic explanation, but it is the explanation, the articulation, the verbal expression of what we have actually already grasped when we love our neighbor.

In conclusion, I refer to what I tried to allude to at the beginning. How can we, as witnesses to the truth of the love of God, convince people that there truly exists what we confess in faith? God appears to be distant. But we can do one thing: we can love in a selfless way and try to say to people, "See, by what you are doing, you have already begun to love God." We can live this out before people and show them the one convincing and possible point of departure for all of Christianity, namely: the love of our neighbor. When we do so, we have done what we are meant to do in our lives; we have given witness to the first and last basic testimony of Christianity. We will still have to say much else from the pulpit, in the classroom, and in other places about Christianity; but when this entire message does not begin with the witness of one's deed and one's own life that says that we have decided to love our neighbor in a selfless way, then the rest of our talk remains unintelligible, since the first key word is missing, the word that could convince people of today.

If we want to be messengers of God and of God's love, then we might simply do this: love our neighbor in life, in caring, in patience, in forgiveness, in helping. Then we will not only have begun with authentic Christianity but we will have lived it from its essence and core; and then it can unfold from there in us and become a witness to God's love in Jesus Christ for us, so that people will believe that God exists, since they have experienced his love in our neighborly love of God's people.

BEAR WITH ONE ANOTHER
AND FORGIVE EACH ANOTHER
Colossians 3:12–17

As God's chosen ones, holy and beloved, clothe yourselves with compassion, kindness, humility, meekness, and patience. Bear with one another and, if anyone has a complaint against another, forgive each other; just as the Lord has forgiven you, so you also must forgive. Above all, clothe yourselves with love, which binds everything together in perfect harmony. And let the peace of Christ rule in your hearts, to which indeed you were called in the one body. And be thankful. Let the word of Christ dwell in you richly; teach and admonish one another in all wisdom; and with gratitude in your hearts sing psalms, hymns, and spiritual songs to God. And whatever you do, in word or deed, do everything in the name of the Lord Jesus, giving thanks to God the Father through him.

We are the church to whom Paul writes, since he wrote to a church he did not know and so could only say what he would say to all churches. In the first part of the letter, the apostle praises the great honor of the eternal son of God, who as the image of God is before and above all powers and is as the risen one the beginning of the blessed end of our own history, the head of the church, which is us, who have found through him the freedom in God above all earthly powers and principalities. In the second part of the letter, Paul draws the conclusion resulting from these observations about the Christian life. And part of this conclusion is the double paragraph of six verses on which this meditation is based. The text is about how we as Christians should live when we have been reached by faith in God through Christ.

At first, everything related to the lifestyle of the individual and of the church appears very simple and clear. Who would object to the recommendation to practice true compassion, kindness, humility, meekness, patience—bearing with one another and forgiving each other—love, peace, gratitude, mutual teaching in Christian wisdom by the call of Christ's word? It almost looks as if these ideals are, at least on the surface, something to be taken for granted; they appear like humanistic attitudes, which we share with all people who are mature and good-willed.

But when we let these words truly sink in, when they penetrate the façade of our status quo morality, then things change. Perhaps our name is listed as a donor for a good cause or we are wearing a pin on our lapel that protects us from the continued clanking of the tin cup, but do we have compassion at the bottom of our heart? We have adapted our life to our environment because it is the best way to permit our egotism to live on. But do we really have kindness, humility, meekness, and patience of heart in their truest form? We avoid conflict. But do we bear with one another, so that others will know that we are at least partially carrying their burden? Have we ever silently yet truly forgiven someone who has done us wrong? Are we those who are loving or those who have become hardened by life? Are we so-called realists who no longer dare give their disappointed hearts to another? Have our hearts been locked into deep resignation, instead of being lodged in the peace of God who is full of joy, freedom, and living hope? Are we grateful, or have we simply come to terms with the way things are? Do we still manage to say a kind word to another out of true empathy? Can our heart still sing?

When we truly hear the words of the apostle, a deadly fear comes over our heart, this heart that is frozen and dead, that resembles a viper's nest of selfishness and is cunningly covered up by our repressed consciousness so that the horrid ditch we carry within us is precariously concealed.

Now frightened, we continue reading the text. And suddenly we realize that it is not calling on the ideals of our own heart but on ideals given to us by God in Christ, so that we are enabled to meet them. We need to keep in mind that Paul is addressing here God's chosen ones, saints and beloved. And he demands of them the kind of forgiveness that has its origin in our being forgiven by the *Lord*; he talks of *God's* peace, of the power of the word of *Christ*, of singing in the spirit of *God*, of doing in the name of the *Lord Jesus*, which is the empowerment and freedom we receive through the *Lord*. The apostle assumes that it is possible that we as individuals and as a community— we who are poor sinners and continually have to try anew—can do what he is asking for. But what he is asking for comes from God through God's grace by faith; *God* does the work of setting us free in love.

Where is this work of God and his powerfully liberating gift that pulls us out of the ditch of our evil, helplessly suffocating heart? When we ask like this, when we want to step back from ourselves and from God by raising questions in order to scrutinize in a detached manner whether God and his spirit are managing to deliver us from ourselves, then we are already taking the wrong position, a position where nothing about us is going to change. We experience grace only when we do not demand that it give us a prior introduction; rather, we simply start with ourselves, we take ourselves the way we are, we allow ourselves to be told unconditionally "to put on" this or that, we start to walk without asking whether we are allowed to do so, we jump while assuming we will fall into the abyss of our own powerlessness, we push ourselves and make ever new desperate attempts, we allow God to give us the true disposition of heart without which all labor would come to nothing, the nothing, though, that we are able to do.

And so, the text meets us a third time and appears again the way it did at the beginning: like a call to proper ethical behavior, to kindness, patience, peacefulness, the serenity of a singing heart and all the other things without which everyday life would end up in a dead-end street. But this sober call to a way of living out our everyday life comes to us now as the word of grace, which supplies from its end what is called for, which opens up our everyday life to a never-ending freedom, to the realm of God's glory; it is the word of grace that makes possible the continuation of God's own work in us. But, to be precise, this word of grace is the sober imperative of everyday life, which demands in an almost crass and domineering way that we squeeze from our tired and evil hearts a dutiful compliance with what is expected of us, since only when we try to obey do we realize and accept our own powerlessness and the power of God's grace and through this realization and this acceptance become God's saints, God's chosen ones, and God's beloved.

Thus, our text is both a word of judgment and a word of encouragement to us Christians who live today in diaspora, meaning among people who think they cannot accept the Christian message as the guiding light for their life. What is the most important thing that we need to show them, what is the first testimony we owe them if we diaspora Christians are not to bring guilt upon ourselves before God and them? We are to prove ourselves in everyday life by a strength that does not come from us but from God. What one takes most for granted is precisely the hardest to do; this is what Paul says to us in this text. We prove ourselves before others while aware that what we do in the name of Christ is mirrored to us by those who are not Christians or think they are not, so that they judge and accuse us, unaware, just as we are unaware, that their response to what we are doing or should be doing is the result of grace: practicing love, patience, compassion, peace. When we do things with this awareness, our actions can be a true witness to the power of grace, which is at work where it wills and is no respecter of persons.

Our heart is weak and cowardly and always overtaxed by what the word of God demands of us. But God can supply us with what he demands of us. For that reason, we celebrate the Lord's Supper. Here we proclaim his death that frees us into the freedom of the children of God; here we submit to the law of his crucifixion in which ultimate human powerlessness is offered in obedience and becomes the event and the revelation of the power of God; here we receive the body of the Lord that was given for us, so that we who receive it in faith are no longer left to fend for ourselves in weakness but may receive the living mercy of God, which ensures that we will be able to make a start in doing our duty in everyday life. In this very ordinary duty that is unconditionally accepted lies death at its deepest yet most unconcealed level; here is sacrifice without a reward, renunciation without a word spoken, courage that demands one's all and seemingly offers nothing in return, hence a dying, a letting go, a silent acceptance. Those who are enabled to do so and to suffer accordingly that which comes to them from an unknown spring are dying with Christ, whether they know it or not. Since we know it by faith, we celebrate the Lord's Supper, where he himself accepted his own death. It is a terrible thing to place oneself beneath the cross of the one who, when giving his life into the hands of God, said that his God had deserted him. But here alone is the burning bush of thorns that brings salvation and love.

THE ONE SPIRIT—THE MANY GIFTS

NON-BELIEVING CHRISTIANS
AND CHRISTIAN NON-BELIEVERS
Matthew 8:1–13

The Lord was sent first of all to the lost sheep of the house of Israel. These people were a chosen people, the covenant people of God, the property of their Father. But when the Son came into their possession, his own did not receive him. The "patriotism" of this people should have enabled them to remain true to their faith in God and God's word, even if this word was now a new one. But the word become flesh did not find such faith. These people thought that their relationship with God had been firmly settled long ago and that there was nothing that needed changing; they thought that their covenant with God was a good reason for not needing to let God come any closer, their former obedience making it unnecessary for them to have to continue to listen to what God wanted to say.

Among the people with faith in the Father, the Son did not get a hearing because they thought they were already "faithful" enough. The Son found faith in the centurion of the nonbelieving occupational force. That caused surprise in the one who already knew everything. Throughout his entire life, this surprise was never far from the heart of the Son of Man (along with dismay that many who appeared to be outsiders were in reality insiders, while the original residents of the kingdom were thrown out into utter darkness); surprise at finding that unconditional faith often comes easier to "non-believers" than to those who have always "believed," that heaven witnesses true penance more often among sinners than among those who think they no longer have need of it.

All of this is still true today. The borders of the kingdom of God do not necessarily coincide with the borders of denominational lines or those that divide "practicing" from "non-practicing" Catholics. This does not mean that God would not want us to be Catholics and "practicing" ones at that. But among Catholics, not all are truly children of the kingdom. The book of life does not simply contain information based on church statistics, the parish register, and the membership rolls of Catholic organizations.

We will always have to keep this in mind, as obvious as it seems in theory and from general observation. Not everyone who says "Lord, Lord" enters the kingdom of heaven. The "practicing Catholic" who truly qualifies for heavenly admittance has to practice the faith not only in church but also in life in a way that shows patience, modesty, neighborly love, honesty, and all those virtues in which the children of the world seem to be outdoing us by far. Orthodoxy and a faith that truly justifies are two different things. Beneath the clean outer garment could be hiding a heart that lacks God and true love. Church membership alone is not yet true Christianity. In fact, orthodoxy, civil propriety, and church loyalty can involve a danger, the danger of self-righteousness and pious hypocrisy. Everyone tries to cover up some evil ambition with good works. It may be true that we sometimes confess to failure, but only under the condition that others don't take our confession too seriously. When we are good, we take that to mean that we do not need to become better. We are among the people who frequent the confessional booth believing that by admitting to their mistakes they have no need to work on them. We make sacrifices, but mostly they are a substitute for what we should truly sacrifice. When a call goes out for penance, we think of others who need it, instead of ourselves. When our conscience grows too uncomfortable, we preach to and exhort others. In short: somewhere, we are all non-believing Christians, people who withhold from the Lord their faith. The Lord still is walking among his people and must be amazed at how little faith he finds there.

We would do well to look for the "Christian non-believer," that is, for the person who is near God without knowing it and whose view is obstructed by the shadow we ourselves cast. From beginning to end, people are entering the kingdom of God by way of roads that are not officially marked on the map. When we meet such people, they should come to realize through us that the official paths on which *we* walk are the sure and the shorter ones.

PEOPLE AS PROPHETS AND THE CHURCH

The church is confronted with ever new tasks. These tasks come about because of changing historical conditions, and because God himself wants to see the church grow and to show forth the wealth of its hidden life in ever new shapes and forms. The people who are the first to recognize the church's new tasks—who are urging that these tasks be undertaken and are even tackling them masterfully themselves—are certainly not only the church's ordained shepherds, such as bishops and popes. The call for new directions, issued by God's providence, can also come and has certainly come in the past through "the small people" in God's kingdom, the uneducated and the poor, children, those who are secretly praying and doing penance, in short, people who are prophetic, who are driven by the "Spirit that blows where it wills" and who address the church by the message of their life, their example, and their word.

When God's spirit awakens such people, there comes into being a strange mutuality between them and the church. On the one hand, the church is not permitted to "snuff out" their "spirit." The church, including its official shepherds, is called, rather, to be open to the message of the prophets, to pray for them, to receive from them its marching orders at any given time in history.

This has happened again and again, and throughout history we have seen numerous examples of it. Benedict of Nursia was not a priest and yet, moved by the "pneuma" or spirit of wisdom and discretion, he became the father of monasticism, which helped the church and ancient culture make the transition to the new era of the Germanic Middle Ages. The nun Juliana of Lüttich, who died without seeing her goal achieved, was nevertheless the clear inspiration for the introduction of the feast of Corpus Christi. The poor mendicant Francis of Assisi was recognized by Pope Innocent in a dream as the critical support that the church needed. And it should not remain a dream only. Church history names many people without "office and honor" as those who inspired or carried out new movements and events in the church: Antony and Pachomius, the early fathers of monasticism; Catherine of Siena, the one who put an end to the papacy's exile at Avignon; Joan of Arc; Teresa of Avila, the great teacher of modern mysticism; Mary Ward, the patient pioneer of modern women's orders; Margaret Mary Alacoque, the prophetess of the veneration of the Heart of Jesus; Bernadette, the saint of Lourdes, and many others.

On the other hand, such prophetic people are single members of the church and their gift of grace is always only one limited "part" of the many gifts of grace that the one spirit distributes among the church's members, so that the gifts in others need to be acknowledged as well. Spiritual gifts in the church include careful critique, sober theological reflection, recognition of the danger of one-sidedness and narrowness of view. Prophetic people have to remain subject to the teaching and pastoral office of the "official" church. Whether they do so at all, whether they do it gladly, faithfully, unconditionally, becomes the test of whether their spirit is truly from God. When people are genuinely prompted by the spirit of God, they are humble, afraid of being mistaken, aware that only the teaching and pastoral office of the church and the whole church's sound "instinct" can protect them in the long run from the danger of presuming that their own human, yet quite devout, passion has as its origin the Holy Spirit.

There is no shortage of examples to show the importance of the church's critique of "prophetic" people. Among the "visions" of St. Hildegard of Bingen, of St. Elisabeth of Schönau, of St. Birgitta of Sweden, of St. Francisca Romana are found some odd errors, which these saints presumed to be revelations and sometimes sought to impose on their contemporaries, including their bishops, with rather authoritative-sounding words. For example, St. Bernard of Clairvaux predicted the success of the second crusade, which he had recommended, and he lived to see its failure. At critical junctures in church history, such as around the year 1000, or at the end of the Middle Ages, or when the church state was eliminated, predictions about the future frequently circulated—predictions that never came to pass. Before he died, St. Francis imposed on his brothers the stricture to add absolutely no explanations to his rule and to seek no papal clarifications, thus leading to a grave crisis in the young order, a crisis that could be handled only through the wisdom and courage of St. Anthony, who requested—against the specific instructions of his father in the faith—a papal resolution on the rule. The great apostle of eastern Germany, Norbert of Xanten (d. 1134), believed that he knew by special revelation and despite St. Bernard's protests that the antichrist would appear during his own lifetime. St. Catherine of Siena believed that she knew by revelation that the Blessed Virgin had not been conceived immaculately. St. Vincent Ferrer (d. 1419) predicted the imminent end of the world by referring to a special revelation of his and to the miracles he had performed. The blessed Alanus de Rupe (d. 1475), who was a great champion of the rosary, declared the most impossible fantasies (such as the rosary's origin in apostolic times) as revelations he had received: "All these things," he said, "I attest to and declare to be based on my faith in the Holy Trinity. May I be damned if I have departed from the path of truth." He was wrong, but he is not damned. The "great revelation" of St. Margaret Mary is, according to the opinion of reputable theologians, rather questionable in the way the saint presents it. The visionary St. Catherine Labouré, who was the inspiration for the "wonderworking medal," also offered revelations that turned out to be erroneous, as she herself later honestly and humbly admitted. Even certain predictions (about the end of the World War, etc.) and theological statements by the children of Fatima can be regarded with justified skepticism, since they do not change the core of the message of Fatima.

These and other similar examples show that even saintly people and those who are a blessing to the church by their gifts of grace can still be subject to error and to the influence of their age; they are not able on their own to clearly distinguish between the leadings of the Holy Spirit and their personal contributions, something that only the spirit in the office of the church can do. The difficulty of "discerning the spirits" (which in itself is a gift of God's grace) should not make us impatient or hasty. Neither gullibility nor covert or open animosity toward "new" influences that arise through the prophetic spirit in the church is the right attitude. While we should hear the admonition to penance and prayer, which can never be too loud and is the well-justified central theme of the newest revelations, we would be lacking the spiritual gift of discernment if we rejected any warning of caution and of one-sidedness, any extended scrutiny by the church, any examination of new revelations by the standards of sound doctrinal and pastoral theology by viewing such actions as expressions of an unbelieving rationalism. There are enough events in recent history that would commend caution and testing and there are enough people among the devout who need to be told that obedience to the church and sober theological teaching are critical for determining whether the spirit they are trying to introduce to the church is truly from God. Only by submission to the church is there the guarantee that the "prophetic" activity of those called to it will bear good fruit.

ON NOT AVOIDING DECISIONS

Christian life today is filled with principles and general norms and with few imperatives, demands, or concrete instructions. Not that one could ever have too many principles, and, when they are correct, it is appropriate that they should be made known and preached about. It is also true that much would be gained if these proclaimed principles were also being followed and if it were evident that the principles remain valid even in those cases in which following them might bring about disaster.

Still, those who proclaim these principles should also reflect on why they find such little hearing. If they say: It is because this is the hour of darkness and of the power of evil, then they will have to explain why darkness and evil should be so much greater now than before and they should be less inclined to discard the "former truths" and "unchangeable norms." If they say what is actually more important and more correct, namely, that a changing time with its new conditions creates new problems and difficulties that can be tackled only gradually and patiently, they will have to explain whether it is possible to adjust the new conditions and situations, to create an environment in which these principles can be realized, or whether they prefer to draft again new principles for changed times, rather than imperatives. Considered from this angle, what remains true is this: The more doctrinal proclamation of principles should be accompanied by the proclamation of imperatives.

Nevertheless, one has to be clear: The imperatives cannot be principles yet again, as happens in our homilies and our proclamations concerning the positions of the church and its members with regard to the immediate questions and decisions in the lives of individuals and the nation. This is why our words sound so traditional and boring, so cheap and almost hollow. In their essence, they are not, for principles beg to be proclaimed. But people tend to look for imperatives and will unconsciously pay attention to what is proclaimed as if it were an imperative (a mistake also often mistakenly made by those who do the proclaiming).

People are actually correct in their expectation. Listeners are to act, to do something concrete, in which the normative, essential, and "eternally true" can be realized. But then they hear mostly only the idea instead of the concrete suggestion, the abstract principle instead of the visually concrete realization. Therefore, we give the impression of wanting to restore something, and we defend this by saying that the time of great "movements" (such as those of the 1920s) is over. Our speech is too tentative, terribly outdated, and level-headed. Everything is correct, but everything is a little sterile. There is no simple and clear tenet. Everything is too much about the golden mean. One keeps safely in the middle of the road and anxiously avoids the ditches to either side; yet, the cart is stuck. One is proud of the Catholic synthesis of principles that are hard to refute and sometimes seem to be mutually exclusive. But one easily forgets to ask how this balanced system of reconciling principles is to look in practice, for it is impossible that every single perspective of the world that is true and worthy of consideration can have equal weight. One will have to choose, to select a certain individualized "dosage."

The fact is that finite people cannot deduce from one single principle what they should do, regardless of how much one tries to "raise" the complexities of human nature, human responsibility, and human modes of being to ever higher and richer unifying norms. Invariably, people have a multitude of principles. Fair consideration of these principles requires a decision and for that one needs an imperative. Yet, the imperative is what precisely is missing, because only the old imperatives are being offered, those that have already become abstract principles, or the imperatives are wrong, meaning that they have lost their historical relevance, as when one longs for the good old days (which could not actually have been so ideal, given that they were transformed into what we have today). We will have to bypass elaborating on the reasons why in today's Catholic Germany imperatives are missing. But when one is honest, one will still have to admit: the mood among Christians is low, fairly bored, without energy. One does not even argue anymore; one cultivates consensus by avoiding difficult questions; one glosses over and evens things out by employing administrative solutions and thinks that thereby all problems are solved. One is hard pressed to explain to common people what new developments—apart from maintenance of the status quo and responding to certain difficult moral demands and rejecting communism—we desire, how we envision the future, not the one that is to come (since the future has already begun) but the future we want to see come to pass, for which we work and fight. If one wants to object, one might regard the current author also as one of the common people and acknowledge that there are clearly people for whom the imperative has not been made concrete enough.

By looking at some of the most recent national annual Catholic conferences (*Katholikentage*), one might say (in a manner that is perhaps a little maliciously overstated and aware that there are other aspects to such conferences also) that a few years ago one still wanted something concrete as, for example, at the 1949 conference in Bochum, but today one has become more careful; one wants to see the realization of principles only. To say it in a way that the Ignatian *Exercises* might put it: One chooses the (abstract) goal, rather than the concrete means involving both head and (even more important) heart, by which this ever preliminary, yet concrete goal is to be reached. One should hope that the day will not come too soon when one says, "This and that person at least knew what he or she wanted" or when one flees from sheer boredom and over-saturation, caused by an abundance of freedom and the lack of obligatory imperatives, to the yoke of those who have impera-tives, though false or short-sighted ones. It almost looks as if for that or similar reasons the countries of the Eastern hemi-sphere (perhaps only to a small, yet no less important degree) have slowly stopped envying us in the West. And yet, we con-tinue to face invariably new and difficult choices, so that keen Christian thinkers and courageous hearts (each in their own way) should feel compelled not to have only principles but also imperatives, not only a Catholic faith but also a Christian "worldview," if by worldview we mean not the mere sum of correct principles (like natural law, mainly), but the sum total of right and historically valid imperatives.

In the last few centuries, Christians have, rather surpris-ingly, come to represent conservative principles. Hence, it is little wonder that they take too much for granted the impera-tive that they themselves live by and avoid discussing it in de-tail; consequently, they ascribe the other remaining principles to their "revolutionary" opponents because one can prove these principles with certainty and one hopes with less cer-tainty to have thereby also defended the old imperatives. Since Christians are on the defensive, they are inclined to defend themselves on the basis of what is most certain. However, im-peratives are much more easily called into question than prin-ciples. Moreover, the church's role—its authority—in most in-stances is not to provide imperatives. While the church is to proclaim, for example, the basic moral principles of a given market economy, it should not favor another model that might functionally enhance the current one. The representatives of the official church are more or less aware of this situation. Also, the church has had bad experiences when paying the price for or when defending concrete imperatives, such as "alliance of throne and altar" or "abolish the public bath!" and has grown cautious; it is afraid to formulate slogans that have to be retracted later on. Thus, one withdraws into principles.

This is not to say that Christians—and especially lay people, who are equally part of the church—are relieved of the responsibility of having imperatives that are in agreement with the gospel and the teachings of the church and have, beyond that, what makes up a concrete program of Christian behavior. The fact that the church cannot deliver to them these imperatives wholesale does not mean that Christians can have a clean conscience when they do not have them. At the least in this regard, the church cannot quicken the conscience, since it can only point to behavior that is in clear contradiction of principles, not attack wrong or missing imperatives in the lives of individuals or communities. For example, the church cannot or can only indirectly advise against a certain vocation or marriage, even though either one might be much more devastating in the long run than a certain sin, against which it raises a protest. Hence, one can say quite clearly: To find and advance the imperative is first and foremost the responsibility of lay people and their own apostolate, their own cause and action, in contrast to the goals of the Catholic organization "Catholic Action." Here, lay people are not and cannot be simply receivers of ordinances issued by the hierarchy. They should not expect such ordinances and should not think that the lay apostolate begins only when such ordinances or concrete injunctions are made public, as, for example, by Catholic Action. Here, they cannot expect to receive a concrete "mandate" from the church, but they can receive this mandate from their conscience and from God. Distinguishing between principles and imperatives might offer an answer to the question about the position and role of lay people in the church, the lay apostolate, and the difference between Catholic Action and the action of Catholics. When Christian lay people find imperatives suitable for today and make them concrete, then the church (or Christianity as a whole) is acting through them, for lay people are part of the church, while the church as the authoritative teaching and pastoral office need not become involved. Still, the church needs to see to it by its teaching office, such as through the local chapters of Catholic Action, that Christians avoid thinking they have done their duty simply when living in accordance with the authoritatively pronounced principles of the church.

More than before, Christians should be instructed and trained to find the will of God in areas where the church cannot do so. They should be made aware that we Christians can have the duty to agree on an imperative and not just on principles, even when such an imperative, possibly demanding sacrifice and spiritual discipline, cannot be authoritatively imposed by the teaching office. We should learn that it is strategically smarter at times to highlight a few imperatives than to preach all true principles at once. There is such a thing as the humility that is paired with the courage to be soundly "one-sided." (It is called humility because the risk of embarrassing oneself is greater here than when simply endorsing principles.) We could then endorse these imperatives with much greater confidence, passion, and urgency than is usually the case with us, apart from the great programmatic speeches. Perhaps the self-confidence of the people of Caux could be an example here. Imperatives grow in spirit and heart only where there is the freedom of opinion and inquiry, of dissemination and discussion. According to Pope Pius XII, there needs to be a "public opinion" in the church and its absence would do damage to both shepherd and sheep. One might think that this public opinion is not very active, despite a few pleasant exceptions. The heritage of the past can be defended only by conquering a new future. For that, it will take, among many other and more important things, also imperatives and not only principles.

CHRISTIANS IN THE WORLD ACCORDING TO
THE CHURCH FATHERS

We need to continue asking how Christians who live in the world can concretely practice the ideals of Christianity in their lives. We need to apply and tackle this question in ever new ways because the lay person is to unite the worldly vocation with the otherworldly calling in Jesus Christ. The Christian vocation calls people into the bane and bliss of an earthly task that needs to be taken seriously and is deeply challenging. The Christian calling asks a person to inquire about what lies above, to consider oneself a stranger to this world, to be aware that the form of this entire world will pass away and that it is of little use to gain the world while losing one's soul in the process.

It was a common attitude among early Christians to look for the coming of the Lord, so that the entire patristic era presents us with only a few writings that deal explicitly with the issue of asceticism among the laity. Therefore, the writings of Clement of Alexandria are all the more remarkable in that they probe the connection between the Christian life and the cultural life of antiquity. One will have to recall the ascetic seriousness of early Christians and their ideal of perfection in order to see the importance of such an attempt, one that tries to explicitly sketch the ideal image of the Christian in the world while preserving this ascetic Christian attitude.

The situation at the time was unique and a similar situation would not occur again for a long time: Christianity had become strong and the number of Christians had increased at the turn of the second to the third centuries, so that one could no longer avoid asking about Christianity's relationship to culture, science, and so forth. There also still remained the idealism of the early church, which demanded the best of every Christian. The type of mass Christianity originating with Constantine had not yet sprung up. Only with Constantine were Christian ideals relegated to monasticism, where they would continue to develop further in the monastic environment and would, from there, govern and define for many centuries to come the Christian ideal of perfection, even for those who lived outside the monastery and even for members of the medieval third orders. Clement was ideal for the task: he had traveled widely, was well read and familiar with the religious currents of his time, was a well-rounded resident of a large city, and (most likely) was a family man.

What Clement wanted to do is evident in the formal structure and literary uniqueness of his great trilogy, divided into "an exhortation to the pagans," "the educator," and "miscellanies"; the third functions as "teacher" or as preparation for the teacher (which of the two is irrelevant here). After the conversion of the pagans to Christianity ("exhortation"), there is the moral formation of Christians by the logos as pedagogue ("educator"), then the spiritual education by the logos as teacher ("miscellanies"). As the content of the second part shows, the "educator" has in mind the moral formation of the wealthy, educated, married city dweller, a man who lives an everyday life in his family, his home, and his public occupation. It is this person that Clement wants to turn into the perfect Christian in the context of his own environment. The further formation in the "miscellanies" is aimed at turning him, this same person, in the midst of his environment, into a "gnostic." The spiritual formation of the "miscellanies" builds on the simple Christian faith, since "gnostic" perfection means only bringing to fruition what faith already contains in its basics. However, the gnostic Christian also cultivates the study of philosophy, music, dialectic, and astrology; he reads poets and philosophers. We could say that the gnosis of Clement is a person's full formation, oriented toward the supernatural connectedness with God that ideally incorporates also all natural goods. "There is only one path of truth, but it contains like an eternal river the waters of all its tributaries" (*Stromata* I, 5, 29, 1). Since the "miscellanies" continue to address the topics of the "educator," one sees that while for Clement the ideal and aim of the Christian

is to be a "gnostic," Clement's central theme is the moral formation of the Christian living in the world as described in the "educator." Clement's true topic throughout is how Christians are to
live out their faith in the world. This topic, that of the perfected
Christian living in the world, brings the world home, so to speak,
and is matched also by the literary form of Clement's work: For
the first time in Christian literature, Clement is writing "a literature that is formed by the world, a literature that is like the one
produced by the educated Roman-Greek world of the time" (C.
A. Bernouli). In his thought and writing, Clement fully repre-
sents the "educated" of his time, at home in their literature, their
philosophy, and their ideals, yet still Christian. This sets the stage
for the challenge that Clement sets for himself, namely, to define
the role of the lay Christian and of lay perfection, the integration
of the world into Christian life.

When looking more closely at this challenge and its suggested solution, we are not considering the details of
Clement's answers, nor the degree to which he succeeds. After
all, the model he proposes applies to us only with regard to the
attitude with which one tackles a situation, not to concrete behavior. His "world" and ours are too different to allow for
more than that.

In addressing the challenge, Clement wants to preserve
the eschatological ethos of Christianity. For him, the martyr is
the perfected one and virginity is the "better choice" and ranks
above marriage with regard to salvation. Determining whether
and to what degree his statements about marriage match this
view is not critical here. It appears that Clement also wrote a
separate treatise on chastity and the sacrifice it entails. He
takes a similar position on true poverty.

Still, we can see Clement's fundamental question and attitude when, in discussing such works of Christian perfection as
martyrdom, virginity, and poverty, he distinguishes between a
deep, inner Christian attitude and the actual accomplishment
of these works. He knows that what truly matters lies somehow beyond these typical accomplishments of Christian per-

fection; that it may appear and find expression in them, but that it is not identical with them, and that, in fact, there can be a gap between the inner attitude and these works, which means that the Christian attitude can find concrete expression also in "worldly" life. He knows that all of us are to be martyrs by suffering as well as by our actions, since such an attitude, especially the attitude of love, means surrendering one's self-will to the will of God and a confession of God, which makes people martyrs. The converse is also true: even the ultimate sacrifice in blood martyrdom is for Clement not the decisive criterion of perfection. Also, he knows that celibacy can lead to spiritual drought: without the inner, holy conviction, the celibate person can end up in misanthropy and become devoid of all love.

From this perspective, Clement tries to develop in a positive way the meaning of life for the Christian in the world. However, he not only wants to show to what degree and in what way a worldly life is permissible and can be tolerated, but the fact that worldly life has a positive moral Christian significance and can make a person whole.

In the words of [Clement] Bardenhewer, "no other church author in antiquity...has dealt with the question of earthly possessions as much as Clement." For the first time in Christian literature, Clement points to social aspects: possessions well utilized are a means to connect people more closely, are part of shaping and sustaining society. To him, the categories of rich and poor are not all religious in nature. He regards married life the same way. Here too, his concern is not simply the acceptability of marriage in moral terms, as in the Gnostic views opposing marriage, but with the value of marriage for its Christianizing and perfecting functions. He may not have been quite successful in reconciling the Christian meaning of marriage with the high regard for virginity among Christians, but he still needs to be praised for trying to acknowledge the value of marriage and for the expectations he formulates, thereby raising the moral standards for marriage rather than lowering them. We need not go into detail here either. What is important is only what is basic about his approach. It is the willingness to see marriage from the perspective in which one professes the Lord by one's entire life. "We are to be holy not only in spirit but by our entire behavior, our lifestyle, our body" (*Stromata* III, 6, 47, 1). This statement was directed not at the libertines but at the Encratites [an ascetic sect that forbade marriage] among Christians. A holiness that professes the Lord means not so much the reining in of our bodies as the reality and effectiveness of a holy life. "We enjoy creation with gratitude and an orientation toward higher things" . . . "Created is celibacy, created is the world. Both [the celibate and the noncelibate] ought to give thanks for the state in which they live, as long as they know that for which they live" . . . "Marriage with a woman creates a house for the Lord" (*Stromata* III, 14, 95, 3; 18, 105, 1; 18, 108, 2).

This is how Clement looks at the entire cultural life of his time: bath and sports, clothes, jewelry, ointments and wreaths, laughing and talking, home goods, participation in banquets, eating and drinking, sleeping, shoes, beauty, interchange, and so forth. These subjects already indicate what is important to him: the interior Christianizing of life in the world. In all things, Clement appears as the man aware of the freedom of the Christian, not as one leaving the world behind as a worldly thing, but as one who realizes that while the Christian is not of the world, the Christian does not flee the world into a lofty spirituality but, instead, brings this world—as the creation of the God who has raised the cross there—home to God.

One can see that Clement was intentional about this because, by his definition, the true gnostic—the perfected Christian—is both "worldly and other-worldly" at once. For Clement, the truly devout person is the one "who serves God in human affairs beautifully and without reproach" (*Stromota* VII, 1, 3, 4). The perfected Christian is not merely worldly but is also not merely condemning, in the Gnostic sense, of what is not "pneumatical" or otherworldly. He is both. With that, Clement expresses the metaphysical formula of Christian life in its ancient form and in the form that needs to be ever newly adapted.

Clement's explicit and broad attempt in this regard is unique in the patristic era. Even Origen, of greater stature than Clement, is much less favorably and positively inclined toward the world, paving the way by his own asceticism for the monastic lifestyle yet to come. In general, the second half of the third century was a strangely unfruitful period in patristic literature. Then, in the first half of the fourth century, there began, amidst the church of the empire with its lowered standards for the masses, the great flowering of monasticism, which started out in Egypt, spread quickly throughout the entire East, and became influential in the Western church during the second half of the fourth century.

We need not elaborate on the factors that led to the extraordinarily sweeping development of monasticism, which turned the ascetics and virgins of the church who had been living modestly in the Christian community during the first three centuries into "orders," then extended this lifestyle (or a good portion of it, at least) to clerics, so that both of these groups began to be distinguished over against "lay Christians," who were a group excluded and separate from the leading people of God, due to the church's hierarchical structure and the ideals of Christian life. This development occurred very quickly. For example, whenever John Chrysostom preached on the perfected Christian life, his audience would protest, saying: But we are not monks! Already at that time, lay people had the incorrect notion that they belonged to that group of Christians that was less strictly obligated to follow Christian ideals. Conversely, Christian perfection and monasticism became almost identical in meaning.

In Basil's writings, the monk and the Christian are nearly the same. When Chrysostom wants to commend the ideals of a perfected Christian marriage, he knows of no higher praise than to place married life a little below the life of monks. When the parable of the thirty-, sixty-, and hundred-fold return is interpreted to mean the three stations in life, namely marriage, widowhood, and virginity, it seems a little too simplistic for our taste. When Jerome writes about the education of girls, it becomes an instruction on how to raise a prospective nun. According to the Pseudo-Areopagite, monks receive a special place in the "church hierarchy," a place that is above that of other lay people. In the pilgrim's legend in which a holy monk receives the revelation that he is no more perfect than a certain humble lay person in his or her hidden holiness, it most frequently happens (with one praiseworthy exception) that the lay person eventually becomes a monk or nun, becomes externally what he or she had been all along internally from the viewpoint of the legend's author.

In biographies, such as that of Melania the Younger, or in the novel about Nilus of Sinai, the happy ending to a Christian marriage takes place when both husband and wife join the monastery. In Augustine, not to speak of Jerome, lay people are most definitely viewed as "the weaker ones." As already mentioned, one cannot examine here in greater detail the degree to which such perspectives in their rather blunt formulation describe solely the Christian view that prefers the ascetic life over life in the world rather than seeing the ascetic life as an individual badge of moral honor or acknowledging the individual's potential "calling" to a life in the world; the degree to which these perspectives reflect real life and the actual conditions at the time; the degree to which they are a result, not of a Christian attitude, but of the pessimism of late antiquity and a Hellenistic animosity toward the body, a view that has always regarded the "spirit" and a spiritual emphasis to be the more Christian way. After all, monasticism was considered a "philosophy" too. These examples show that in the late patristic era the ideals of Christian life in the world were seen from the perspective of monasticism, which meant that the formulation of a lay morality and perfection was neglected, as were the unique values of the Christian life in the world.

This is not to say that the flowering of early Christian monasticism completely blocked the intentional development of lay perfection. That would be one-sided, even if we were to ignore the questions regarding whether and to what degree a desire for it existed back then. There is no doubt that monasticism greatly preserved and spurred on the liveliness of Christian ideals and hence had a formative influence upon lay Christianity as well. There can be little doubt that the radicalism by which the numerous holy representatives modeled Christian life to a tired, aging cultural world had to be a unique blessing to vast numbers of average Christians. When ascetic ideals were opposed, one finds at least as much protest against monasticism coming from clerical circles as from the laity, which means opposition was not solely a lay matter. When monasticism modeled a life of manual labor to the world of antiquity and showed that this was part of the ideal Christian life, it provided the greatest service to the culture and ethos of lay Christianity. The first patristic praise of physical labor over against antiquity's disdain of a life of labor is Augustine's "About the Labor of Monks."

Apart from all that, there is evidence that in the high patristic era one did not forget that even the lay person—just as any Christian—was called to perfection and was enabled and obligated to practice it in his or her own unique way. A few examples will have to suffice here.

One need only point briefly to the lay martyrs, even though they are not exactly lay people any longer, since, as martyrs, they become "saints" and their martyrdom lets the distinction of their station in life disappear. Among them, we find holy soldiers and workmen, physicians, philosophers, married couples, mothers with children, the great of the earth, and slaves. They show by their mere presence that the great ones in the kingdom of God are chosen from all trades and professions, and hence that they are already sanctified in their worldly state. Occasionally, this is also explicitly affirmed by blood witnesses such as the holy martyrs Crispinus and Crispinianus, who as shoemakers were engaged in benevolent causes, or by the diligent gardener Phokas of Sinope. The

"four holy crowned ones" are explicitly praised for the dili-
gence shown at their trade, an attitude resulting from the
Christian ethic of work. Accordingly, an ancient martyrs' legend speaks of "*statio artis facta est domus orationis*," or "the place
where work is done as the house of prayer." The numerous
holy physicians, who are honored as *anargyoi*, as those treating
patients for free, may also be mentioned here.

Compared to the many holy bishops, priests, monks, and
virgins we know of, there are only few known "saints" of the
time who were and remained lay people: a few holy workmen
and physicians of whom we know little more than their holy
life and their profession (even though that is significant); a few
fathers or mothers who were honored or venerated as saints,
some to whom attention was drawn by a great holy son, as in
the case of Monica, the mother of Augustine, the parents—
and grandparents—of St. Basil, the mother of St. John
Chrysostom; and finally the saints who were called to become
bishops on account of their exemplary life as lay people. This
is not surprising.

Since back then the ideal of the saints was (for good reason)
strongly, yet a little too directly, oriented to the martyr's ideal,
it is understandable that one would see a parallel to these holy
witnesses first and foremost in the lives of hermits and monks,
whose asceticism was considered almost exclusively a substitute
for martyrdom. It is also not surprising that those considered
next were religious leaders of nations, namely bishops, since in
those days it was much easier than today for someone of religious importance—regardless of the person's profession and
marital status—to become a bishop. One can think of people
like Gregory the Wonderworker, Ambrose, Paulinus of Nola,
Martin of Tours, Parthenius of Lampsacus, and others.

Either in theory or by the concrete evidence of glowing
examples, one never forgot that saintliness in the world could
exist and had to exist. We have already mentioned the pilgrim's
legend, numerous variations of which appear in monastic literature. Certainly widely read, it maintained awareness that

"Truly, whether virgin or wife, whether monk or lay person, God grants by his own good pleasure the Holy Spirit to each" (*Vitae Patrum* VI, 3, n. 17).

The main preacher of Christian lay perfection was John Chrysostom. While one of the most fervent advocates of monasticism, he never forgot that each Christian is to become perfect. He was disturbed when, as mentioned earlier, his sermons about the ideals of Christian life produced repeatedly the same trite objection: "But we are not monks!" Both the ascetic and the Christian in the world are subject to the same law of Christ; the Sermon on the Mount is aimed equally at all. The married Christian can practice virtue to the same degree that a monk can by praying and reading scripture (a favorite topic of this great preacher!); in short, one is to be a Christian as if one were a monk. Ultimately, the moral value of a life is measured by love, and without love even poverty and martyrdom are worthless. Christian perfection consists largely in perfected love, which springs from a true faith and finds expression in a life that is in harmony with God's commandments. With that, a program is drawn up that applies to everybody. Chrysostom's lifelong concern was Christian perfection among all and a holiness that was not the monopoly of people with a certain station in life. Those wishing to learn about his ideals of marriage might read, for example, his Homily 20, which is on the letter to the Ephesians. It contains an entire ethical code on Christian marriage.

Finally, one needs to consider also the patristic letters. This literature shows that even back then one wrote "heart-to-heart" letters to lay people who deeply desired a perfected Christian life. Of course, there are only a few such letters, naturally addressed almost exclusively to prominent people with whom the author maintained close personal ties. For the most part, these letters are responses to inquiries, letters of thanks, or letters of exhortation. Since the reason for their writing is incidental, these pastoral care letters address only partial aspects of the spiritual life. The important point about them is not that they identify the inner spiritual attitude of Christians or can justify such an attitude theologically. Everything fundamental is largely presupposed, so that one finds addressed here only the specific questions of what the Christian faith should look like in real life. For that reason, we would search in vain for a theoretical reflection on the ascetic life of lay people in general or its individual areas. Instead, we find among valuable exhortations and hints rather detailed instructions about married life, prayer, and other issues that will be of ongoing and lively interest to those wishing to translate their faith into practice. The words in these letters attest to a wealth of life experience, theological wisdom, and a high personal ethic, and they remain for us an interesting testimony to early Christian piety and a source of valuable inspiration.

THE DIVINE MYSTERY OF MARRIAGE

This mystery is great, and I mention it in connection with Christ and his church" (Eph 5:32). Over the last few decades, Catholic literature and preaching on marriage have not grown tired of quoting and elaborating on this scripture passage by the apostle Paul. Yet its interpretations were and are mostly a simple transposing of the mystery of Christ/ church into the loving communion and union between man and woman without showing more concretely how one encounters in this mystery the loving movement of people from below and of God from above, so that one flows into the heart of God and the other into the heart of people.

Considered solely from the human perspective, the holy and bold undertaking of beginning a joint life of love and fidelity reaches into the mystery of God. When in the freedom of their existence people have free reign over themselves, when they dare to entrust their heart, life, fate, and eternal dignity to another, thus revealing themselves to the ever mysteriously new, unknown, and hidden mystery of another, it is possible that such an undertaking, which happens so frequently that it may look rather ordinary and almost trite on the surface, still is what it appears to be to the lovers: the unique miracle of love. And such a miracle borders on God, for it encompasses the entire person and his or her entire destiny. To take such an action in freedom always means, regardless of whether one knows it, the drawing near and enduring presence of the perhaps unnamed, silent, all-encompassing and sheltering, rescuing and blessing partner we call God. This is because such an undertaking is without boundaries, points to infinity and the unconditional, and is possible only in the unlimited fullness of the human spirit, which invariably points to God. In true personal love, there is always something unconditional that points beyond the conditional of the lovers; when they truly love, they continually grow beyond themselves, taking part in a movement that no longer has its aim in the nameable finite.

That which is silently invoked in such love and lies at an infinite distance can ultimately only be named God. God is the granter of eternal love; he is the custodian of the person's dignity, which is given away in love and entrusted to another fallible and finite person; he is the fulfillment of the infinite promise that is inherent in love, yet this love could not reach its own fulfillment completely even if it wanted to. God is the immeasurable depth (by grace) of the other without which each person would ultimately appear hollow and void. He is the infinite width where, upon entering, one finds the room in which to carry out of love the burdens that one does not want the other to carry alone, burdens that would be oppressive when carried on one's own. As the one true forgiveness in each of the partners, God stands behind and above each act of forgiveness, without which no love can survive for long. He is sacred fidelity, which one has to love in order to be able to be true to the other. In a word, he is love itself, from which derive all other loves and toward which all other loves have to be open to prevent their becoming a false adventure that ultimately dies of its endlessness.

God's secret partnership in marriage becomes concrete and clear to us only in its sacramental mystery. From the message of faith we know that marriage reaches into the mystery of God in a much more radical way than we could possibly fathom, based on the experience of unconditional human love. The church states that marriage is a sacrament. We take this for granted. But we need to understand what is meant by that statement in order to honor the almost fearsome courage by which one speaks so highly of such a common human act.

Among Christians, marriage is a sacrament. Hence, it bestows grace. Grace does not only mean God's help, so that the marriage partners can be loving and faithful, patient and courageous, selfless and supportive in carrying one another's burdens. Grace does not only mean God's help in fulfilling tasks and duties, which everyone recognizes to be part of this world and acknowledges, at least in theory. Grace means more: Grace means godly life; it means the power of the eternal, participation, pledge, seal and anointing, beginning and ground of the kind of life that is worth living for an entire eternity because it is pulled into the life of God; it means ultimately God himself, who in the infinite fullness of his existence and of his inexpressible grandeur wants to spend himself directly on the spiritual creature.

It is true: All of this is still hidden beneath the veils of faith and hope. It is still incomprehensible and dark and may not yet have risen from the depths of our consciousness to the planes of our trite, everyday experience of life. But all of it exists. And it is what God in the innermost and yet still inaccessible center of our nature has created as the seed of a life of eternity, freedom, and blessed value and is what we denote by the small, dry word "grace." And now we say of grace—which is not simply some everyday help God gives us to act morally—that it increases with the sacrament of marriage. This means that when there is a marriage among us Christians, when there is a sign of the inseparable love raised in this world that also points to the saving love of Christ for his church, grace occurs. It means that there one finds divine life, provided it is not hindered by the death-wielding guilt of the lovers; there begins a new movement that can carry one even deeper into the life of God; there new depths of divine glory break open in the region of the spirit in which God communicates himself as the life of the soul to the human spirit; there love grows to a sweeter gentleness and a stronger fidelity, connecting people to their God; there occurs the one mystery of all existence, yet deeper and more alive, more powerful and more unconditional than before. It is there that one finds God directly communicating with the person's interior.

These are the consuming, bold, and divine statements that can be made about marriage when it is called a sacrament. One says about marriage that it is not only a communion of love between two people but also a communion with God by grace alongside them and in them. There is no doubt that this cannot happen apart from human freedom and without the human "yes." Hence, there is no doubt that lovers will experience this reality only to the degree that they open themselves up to it with believing and faithful hearts. God desires this grace event, so that this encounter with God himself by grace can and should happen also here and now. For this reason, marriage is truly a mystery of God, a piece of divine liturgy in which the mysteries of eternity become salvifically present by its divine celebration.

The liturgy of the marital "yes" leads to the celebration of the holy sacrifice. And that is truly right. The grace of marriage is Christ's grace. It issues from where all grace originates: from the pierced heart of the Savior, who upon the altar of the cross gave himself for the church, his bride, by falling into the eternal darkness of death in trust that thereby he might be placing his own soul into the hands of his Father and releasing it in holy abundance for the salvation of all. From the pierced heart of Christ results all grace, including the grace of marriage without which marriage cannot remain whole and blessed. Therefore, the grace of marriage bears the characteristic of its origin. It is the grace of sacrificial love, the grace of forgiving, carrying, excusing, selfless, pain-concealing love; it is the grace of that love which is true unto death, the grace of that love which is fruitful for life and in death; it is the grace of the love that Paul praises, the love that is merciful, that believes all things, bears all things, hopes all things, endures all things, the love that never ends and without which everything else is brought to nothing. If, therefore, we bring together in sacred celebration before God's holy altar the celebration of such a marital union and the celebration of the highest act of Christ's sacrificial love for his church, then we enter automatically into a prayer for such love and open our hearts to it.

"The God who has called you is faithful and will bring to completion" the Christian life begun in you, says Paul (1 Thess 5:24). A sacrament is actually a part of what completes the Christian life. Therefore and with trust in the power of grace and the divine promise, we may apply this word of the apostle also to the loving communion between spouses. Those who have received the sacrament of marriage are called by God to participate in God's love by loving their spouse. But God is the one who also sustains those who are weak and he effects the divine completion of human marital love. Both husband and wife will have to surrender to him and to the blessed strength of his grace poured out from the heart of the dying Lord if they wish to lend their marital devotion the depth and purity that marriage asks and calls for by its very nature.

THE MYSTERY OF THE SAINTS

FEAST OF HOLY BEGINNINGS
On the Feast of the Immaculate Conception of Mary

Since in the kingdom of God, in the kingdom of love, people come to know things in their own way and everything is intertwined and connected, each of the kingdom's mysteries is immeasurable. One understands these mysteries only when one has understood everything, and this totality is the vastness of the infinite mystery of God. It is the reason one can look at the mystery of the feast of the immaculate conception of Mary from many different angles. And each person is free to choose the way that will be best suited and most fruitful in exploring this divine mystery so as to ultimately arrive at God himself.

We want to look at this feast as one of beginnings. We will consider what beginning is in general, the beginning of the Blessed Virgin, and our beginning.

Beginning in General

The beginning in general is not empty nothingness, insignificance, hollow indefiniteness, the subordinate and the undefined. However, that is how people mostly look at it. They regard everything that is high and perfected (if they are even able to think in those terms and love such things) as stemming from a clever mixture of the cheapest—and equally insignificant —subordinate "basic elements." Yet the true beginning of what leads to the highest perfection is not hollow emptiness but the closed bud, the rich soil of growth that already contains within what it will send out, not as the first and smallest piece at the beginning of life, but as the entirety of evolving history contained in its original beginning.

After all, the beginning in general is God, the fullness of all reality. To say that we have been created out of "nothing" means we are not God; it does not mean that our origin is emptiness and an indifferent indefiniteness, but rather that it is God. And it is God who creates the beginning, which is not the first moment of our time but the basic ground of all of history within the flow of time. That is why the beginning is made only by God; why he is our beginning's mystery that acts on us but cannot be acted upon; why God reveals himself slowly in the course of our history; why he has to be accepted in his own hidden darkness in a trusting, hoping, daring way; why he has to be preserved by holy anamnesis in his elusive mystery and through what he reveals of himself in history. For when God is the remaining ground of existence, carrying everything and not merely what one leaves behind as the past, then he becomes the challenge of life, the content of anamnesis that allows the beginning to be present in holy celebration. That is why we celebrate birthdays, baptismal days, the beginning of Holy Week, all holy days that mark a beginning that has been given to us as people and as Christians. And when we look with hope into the future, we are also looking for the revelation of the beginning; we are encountering in the ending the beginning, in the future the origin out of which history has unfolded. And when we do not reach fulfillment in the end it is only because we have lost sight of the beginning. When the outcome is pure fulfillment, then the beginning had to have been the pure beginning of eternal love. The Gospel of Thomas says: "The disciples said to Jesus: Tell us how our ending will be. Jesus said: Did you already discover the beginning so that now you are asking for the ending? For where the beginning is, there also lies the ending. Blessed are those who will be standing at the beginning, for they will recognize the ending and will not taste death." The historical Jesus certainly did not say this. But when read properly, it is surely true. Jesus viewed the present as deriving from pure beginning, ordained by God and reclaimed by God, since he says: This is not the way it was in the beginning. And when Heidegger says, "Origin always remains future," he is describing the relationship between beginning and fulfillment in the same way as does the historical and the gnostic Jesus. When celebrating a feast of pure beginnings, we should first consider the nature of beginning in general.

The Beginning of the Blessed Virgin

Once we have grasped what beginning means, we will understand that what the church believes about the holy virgin's beginning today is simply a translation of what the church had been originally saying about her and about her salvific relevance to the church. This is true, even though the church may have taken a long time to connect present formulations with the original one, what had developed over time with its original form, the future with its origin, until it could finally arrive at the formulation of 1854. In the case of Mary, God as beginning and the beginning set by God should not be separated because of the disparity that human sin creates. This disparity is permitted on account of Christ, not apart from him and his salvific deed, since even before the world and the world's sin came into being, he is the absolute and unconditional will of God for his world, the pure and most original beginning of the will of God for the material world. Consequently, sin was permitted in the world because it was, at the same time, enveloped by this still-hidden beginning, which from the start was the abundant source of grace, though its fullness became known only gradually as it flowed forth. Thus, Mary belongs to the will of the eternal God, the absolute God, the one who, from the beginning, willed the incarnation of his logos for the sake of containing sin. Mary is part of this enveloping beginning, not what is enveloped by it. Her beginning has been set and she is not the one setting it. She is set as a salvific beginning into the will for the world, into the will of the logos coming into the world and working salvation there. Mary belongs to the act of God by which God contains sin in a saving way, and in the concrete order of this act the incarnate logos cannot be separated from her flesh and her obedience. For this reason also, there does not exist in her the disparity between the God-given beginning of a person and the individual's guilt originating with Adam's deed. Her beginning is pure, innocent, simple, undiluted grace, a deed wrought on the object of salvation itself. From the beginning God loved Mary with an absolute love as the one who says "yes" to his word spoken to the world, since this absolutely willed, unconditionally willed word of grace can be spoken in an absolute way only when it is also heard in absolute obedience and in one's own flesh, namely by Mary. Since God desired her from the beginning to say "yes" and desired this unconditionally, she is in her origin the one doing so and cannot be thought of as one saying "no." She is in her beginning the one full of grace. She is pure for the sake of Christ, the Savior, hence is the moment preceding salvation, so that sin is allowed only for salvation's sake. This beginning is purely ordained by God, a moment in time when God's love for people is still gathered at its origin and not yet dispersed as what has already preceded human guilt and as the love that permits by its power the powerlessness of guilt. Where this love has its beginning in creation's history, there also is the beginning of the blessed virgin; or, better yet, the glory of her pure divine beginning had to be precisely that—beginning. It had to be found by Mary, captured, and painfully experienced. This origin carried within itself the future of her everyday life, of her ordinariness, of her silence, of her sevenfold pain, and of the death of her son and her own self. Only with that was the beginning captured by the future. Only then could the beginning be revealed as pure grace.

Our Beginning

Our beginning is hidden in God. It is set. And only when we have arrived will we fully know what our origin is. For God is complete mystery and what God ordained when setting us into our beginning is still the mystery of his free will concealed in his word of revelation. Yet we can say without negating this mystery that part of our beginning is the earth that God created, our forebears in whose history God acted with wisdom and mercy, Jesus Christ, the church and baptism, time and eternity. Everything is contained there, everything that exists is silently gathered there in the origin of our own existence, and everything else—everything that is unique to each person and characterizes the person as the unique and non-repeatable beginning set by God—is penetrated by it. This includes the heavy and the light, the gentle and the harsh, the deep and the heavenly. Everything is enfolded by God, by his knowledge and his love. Everything is to be accepted. And toward everything we move, so that we experience it all, one thing after another, until the future has caught up with the origin. However, we already know one thing about this beginning through the word of God: the ability to accept belongs to the power of the God-given beginning; and when we accept, we accept pure love and blessedness. Even though the gap between the divine and the human will has been placed in our beginning, and in our beginning we are both those governed by God and those governed by the history of sin, this tension in us is permitted only because it is already enfolded by pure love and divine forgiveness. The more we accept what enfolds us and what belongs to our origin amidst the pain of life and in life-giving death and the more the original can come to light and show itself and is permitted to work its way throughout our life, the more this gap is closed and the original contradiction is resolved. To the same degree, it will become clear to us that we, too, were included in this pure beginning whose feast we celebrate. When the beginning has found itself in fulfillment and has been made complete in the freedom of accepted love, then God will be all in all. Everything, then, belongs to everyone, and the differences, though still present, will have become transfigured and will be part of the blessedness of a unifying love, not of separation. Therefore, this feast is our feast, for it is the feast of the unconditional love in which all of us, each in our own way and depending on where we are, are enclosed.

THOMAS AQUINAS

I

Since we are observing the feast of St. Thomas and, as is appropriate, are remembering and considering the patron saint of theological studies, it might be important to reflect first on the Catholic veneration of saints. This practice is considered a particularly Catholic trait of Western Christianity, and rightly so. However, we need to understand what is meant by the veneration of saints. Then we might realize that, at least in this regard, we are not as Catholic today as we might think. The veneration of saints is not merely the historical remembering of a human and ecclesiastically significant past, but a true and real relationship with a live person who has been perfected and, thus, remains present to us in a powerful way. The veneration of saints entails faith, hope, and love, and is the participation in the kingdom of God that has already begun its process of completion. This is a view with which all of us or at least most of us struggle; we are simply not inclined to see things in this manner nowadays.

In a rather strange way, religion has come to mean for us a focus on God. We view the saints as if they had dissolved into past history and into death because we acknowledge only one absolute mystery, because religion now means to us stepping before the abyss of radical eternity and incomprehensibility, because the dead have become terribly dead and distant to us, because the world of humans has become brittle, terribly finite, and, most of all, ordinary. And while we do not deny their survival in our memory, the saints have virtually been swallowed up and have disappeared in the one word that still is spoken by our religion today, namely, God.

This is actually not Catholic at all, so that the old-fashioned Catholic tradition of venerating the saints still stands before us as a far goal in our religious development, as a higher future. It means that before us still lies the true, real, living appropriation of the fact that the saints are, that they are alive, powerful, near us more than ever; that they are not absorbed into God, but are affirmed by him who is truly the God of the living and not of the dead; that one does not perish by going near God but comes ultimately into one's own fullness and autonomy; that the true God does not need to strip others of power and that, consequently, the veneration of saints is neither a concealed polytheism nor a puerile type of piety that has not yet grasped the majesty and awe-inspiring mystery of God but is, instead, maturity in one's Christian relationship with God. Such maturity knows that the creature does not vanish in the abyss of God when surrendering to him but rather becomes truly alive and present. Such maturity means for the creature finding oneself in God, since one has entered into relationship with God rather than having been dissipated in him. Such maturity places the creature in God, in his perfection, in the finality of God's self-communication toward the creature, so that the finding is a truly religious act belonging to the maturity of one's relationship with God.

What the creature finds in God, what is praiseworthy and recognized as eternally valid in the creature, what is lovingly embraced is, hence, not an imaginary continuation of existence and activity, as if this perfected creature were to come as a demiurge or intermediate being between God and us, but is precisely the eternity of its own time, the irrevocable value of a life lived on earth. Just as the anamnesis of Jesus is both the remembrance of his unique history and the invocation of the risen Lord, it is two distinct moments of one and the same event. If Jesus were not the risen one, his story would have perished in the mists of the past. And if he were not the historical one who came into ultimate being and whose own unique life rests with eternity, he would be called upon only as an idea or an empty name or as an unpredictable, unknown power. The same thing applies to the saints. We call upon these people known to us from their history as those who have been transfigured and whose story is also the story of their perfection.

II

When selecting from the wealth of the spiritual features of St. Thomas a few traits that still are of certain spiritual benefit for us today and by opening ourselves up to them with reverence, we are aware that these selections are haphazard; people should feel free to choose other features or traits that can lend clarity to the image of this saint. With these observations, let us then proceed.

1. Thomas is the concrete and sober one. Anybody who has read a little from his *Summa* will have noticed this. His tone is subtle, restrained, almost quiet, and he does not reach for impressive words. Thomas sees no need to enlarge upon the great subject matter he is discussing by using big words, since doing so is not possible anyway. He hardly betrays a preference for certain theological themes. He is concerned with totality, hence, with each detail. For this reason, he is not blinded by particulars; he always sets out from the perspective of the whole and moves toward it. Since he does not want to impress but rather is impressed by the subject matter, since he is still meditating and appropriating reality for himself by

speaking of this reality to others, he talks almost as if talking to himself, in a quiet, frugal way that is patient with himself and with the subject matter, noble toward his opponents (if he even has them), allowing them to consider the inner breath and spaciousness of his mind. He is the systematic theologian who always is looking at the particular from the perspective of clearly defined ultimate principles. But since he is the concrete one, the particular does not serve him as an occasion to make pronouncements about principles but it is dealt with in a truly loving manner, even if at first glance a consideration of the particular does not seem to fit easily with the great guiding themes of his own thought. This concrete sobriety betrays a concealed awe, a virile respect that pierces the soul, a longing for the eternal light that still shines indirectly, and an aware-ness that even in theology all understanding is truly theologi-cal only to the degree that it shows constant awareness of its preliminary and inadequate nature. In his thinking, Thomas is certainly the concrete and sober one.

2. Thomas has made his theology his spiritual life, and his spiritual life is his theology. In him, there does not yet exist the horrible gap often found in subsequent theological thought between theology and the spiritual life. He thinks theologi-cally because he needs theology as the most fundamental basis for his spiritual life, and he does theology in a way that be-comes truly "existential." His spiritual thought does not revert to a primitive state that would suggest he had never done the-ology, as is evidenced by his eucharistic hymns. He does not believe that the spiritual life develops best and by necessity in the soil of simplicity, intellectual laziness, and spiritual medi-ocrity. It would be unthinkable that he, the theological scholar, would nurture his spiritual life like a simple friar with the third-rate fare of the pious visions of a nun who presents, cer-tainly in good faith, the fantasies of her imagination as the rev-elations of God. Since we mostly study only his *Summa* (and it is deplorable that this is the case), we should not forget that he

understands himself mainly as an interpreter of holy scripture and that to him and others of his time such an undertaking was both academic and spiritual. He writes hymn texts that combine depth, seriousness, and simplicity, and they are his theology and his spiritual life all wrapped into one. Because today's theological books often lack spiritual depth and spiritual books lack theology, there is the danger that we might look at theology as an unpleasant obstacle that needs to be overcome on the way to the priesthood and that later our spiritual life and preaching will draw sustenance from the small, rerouted rivulets of pious secondary literature, rather than from the scriptures and the superior theology of the church fathers and great theologians. In Thomas, theology and the spiritual life are truly still one.

3. Thomas is the mystic who venerates the mystery that cannot be pronounced. He does not think that theology is permitted to speak in imprecise and vague terms because its subject matter is the infinite mystery of God. But neither does he think that the precise speech of theology should lead to the impression that one knows and has captured the mystery of God in the elaborate gyrations of theological definition. Thomas knows that the greatest precision and a sober matter-of-factness have only one purpose when it comes to true theology: to force people out of the visible clarity of their existence into the mystery of God, where they no longer can comprehend but are being apprehended, where they no longer reason but pray, where they do not master but are being mastered.

Only when a theology of rational descriptions negates itself and becomes a theology of captivating incomprehensibility is it actually theology. Otherwise, it remains mere human chatter, even if what is said is true. One need not constantly interpret as figurative speech the words "*Adoro Te devote, latens Deitas, quae sub his figuris vere latitas*" but should rather regard God's hidden nature (*latens*) as the deepest principle of all theological thought and understanding. This is true not only today but in eternity also, where we will know the way we are known and see face-to-face what is regarded, loved, and praised as the eternal mystery, what then enters the heart as such, thereby not becoming smaller but even more incomprehensible and consuming than formerly, when it was expressed in signs and parables. Therefore, it cannot be any different with the "*theologia viatorum*," which needs to be an instruction in the experience of this mystery, albeit a mystery that has drawn close. The lazy one, the one lacking brains and heart, the lackadaisical one should not state that all that is said in theology is like straw, as Thomas said. But if one were to experience fervently and vividly in one's spirit and heart a deadly and piercing pain like that of Thomas, though not, as in his case, resulting from a contemplation of theology and then were to say that everything spoken of in theology is only "*paleae*" or straw, one would not have done theology in the tradition of Thomas. It would be a theology that is smart but not filled with the spirit, and hence it would not be truly Thomistic.

Thomas is alive and he lives his life with God, where that life is completely pure and made valid in utmost purity. And while it is *his* life, it still remains open to the endlessness of God and to the incomprehensible vastness of other callings. Therefore, one can truly say in faith: St. Thomas, pray for me!

THOMAS AQUINAS AS MONK, THEOLOGIAN, AND MYSTIC

The celebration of the feast of St. Thomas Aquinas, the patron saint of theological studies, is not only a spiritual-historical remembering. What we are doing or should be doing here as Christians is also a matter of engaging with the communion of saints. Those in heaven are not dead. They are alive. They live in complete fulfillment, hence in true reality, which is powerful and present. Those who can be called by name are true reality, are what matters more than theoretical principles and abstract theories. The fact that they are, that they are with God, that they love us, that we love them, that they intercede for us who are their brothers and sisters in the unending liturgy of heaven, that the essence of their life remains by their eternal salvation embedded also in the ground of all reality by which history remains, including the history that has occurred after them and is yet to come, that in their very essence they do not belong to the past but are past only in that they have sped ahead of us into the future, the future we have yet to meet: *dominus cum sanctis suis* ("The Lord with his saints")—all of this is more true than we ourselves are.

By comparison to this reality, the temporary aspects of the saints and what is truly gone about them is irrelevant. However, we who are of this earth can recognize the eternal and heavenly dimension of this existing reality of theirs—if such recognition be given to us at all—only by looking back into their past, into their life, which, though in a transfigured way, has entered into the eternal life of God. Otherwise, we would be contemplating only abstract things and not what truly matters: the concrete person, that which is unique and yet eternally valid, that which loves and praises, that which is blessed and saved.

I wish to say three things about Thomas today: He was a monk, a theologian, and a mystic.

Thomas Was a Monk

To say that Thomas was a monk is to say that he was someone who renounced himself. To be sure, this is a harsh and troublesome statement. One can say it also differently: He was a person who let go of the smaller things in order to find the greater things, someone who let go of the world in order to attain to God. But even by saying it in this way, one still has not removed a troubling aspect of Christianity, the fact that even today it is impossible to have it all, that one has to choose, that the dividing line runs straight through one's own personhood, that one has to let go in order to find, that one has to die in order to live, that one has to become poor in order to possess, that in this world one can believe in the God who is everything only by renouncing much. Since Thomas, the holy one, knew this and wanted to live it out, he became a monk, the ordinary one, the poor one, the celibate one, the insignificant one, the one subject to the confines of a religious community. He did not have to do this. His choice of the monastic life was not a social "ladder-climbing" to him, nor was it motivated by resentment over having perhaps missed out on life, nor was it the result of a hollow self-glorification whereby one compensates for personal shortcomings. He had the same type of virile and potent humanity as that of his rowdy brothers, who were convinced that he fit well with them. He was not a religious fanatic who lacked an understanding of, a sense of, and a receptivity to the intoxicating glories of this world. Actually, earthly reality mattered a great deal to him, much more than to the theology before him.

And still, he became a monk. He did so because he desired God and knew himself to be called to this way of life. Since he had the clear faith of the Christian who knows that in the disorderliness of sin, which is the order of this world, and in the order of the cross, this square within a circle that alone is the promise of eternity, there does not exist the possibility of freely and fully taking into one's heart both God and the world, heaven and earth, the blessedness of the human and of the divine. Thus, he made a choice and he decided against the world. He decided, without showing disdain for what he left, and he went knowing that he would find it all again. He gave up in a truly calm and honest way, without the type of twisted fanaticism that is driven by the fantasy that one can live in this world only by renunciation. He knew that in each Christian the path leading to the world intersects with the one on which stands the cross. And since he wanted to be a Christian, he considered it his calling (without imposing the same on others and without becoming confused in his calling by those who disagreed) to become a monk.

The Western priest is, in the deepest theological sense at least, a monk, even though he is not so in a canonical sense and does not need to be. For he is the celibate one, and he is the person who has to a large degree entrusted the disposal of his life to the orders of his bishop, thus being the person who no longer can live his own life. Those wanting to become priests should not be deceived about this. They have to, no, *are allowed to* practice renunciation. In this world, there are a thousand things that are beautiful, animating, wholesome, joyous, and exhilarating and are in no way forbidden to anyone, unless a God-given providence takes them away without asking. The priest has to be able to pass them by and do so with apparent ease, without hatred or resentment, even in a way that does not show that this renunciation is truly costly to him, although only a costly renunciation of what is precious—not a renunciation of what is cheap—is a true act of faith. Such Christian renunciation, such an incarnation of faith that the priest has to model as a testimony to grace in the world, requires practice. It is a practice in the sobriety of everyday life, in the narrow perspective of a seminar, in the dryness of a scholastic course of studies, in the honesty of renouncing the sweet little joys of life that are appropriate only for those called to the married life, in the enduring of an environment that one did not choose, in the obedience that can sacrifice in a quiet and detached fashion one's own opinion to another, perhaps even better, opinion, since ultimately nothing depends on it other than the drive of the self-absorbed self (which needs to die) to be in control. If we want to become priests, we will have to learn in a theological sense to become monks: those who are alone with God, those for whom God is enough, even if it means renouncing other things until there is a new heaven and a new earth.

Thomas Was a Theologian

Thomas was a member of a religious order for which the office of priest and the apostolic mission were not accidental addendums, but by which monasticism tailored itself to fit the priesthood. Hence, he was in accord with monasticism as well as with the priesthood. He was from a strictly theological perspective a priest in the world, a priest for the world. That is the reason he wanted to be a theologian. Since he knew himself sent to proclaim the good news of the gospel, he knew that he had to be a theologian, for one can proclaim in a true-to-life way only what one has made the center of one's own spiritual life. *Contemplata aliis tradere*, giving to others what one has contemplated. *Contemplata*. And if such true contemplation is to be conveyed in preaching, then theology and theological studies are normally the indispensable requisites. That is why Thomas was a theologian. He was a theologian who was always focused on the subject of theology and who had no need to peddle in cheap emotions; someone who could give up the choir office, if necessary, for the sake of studies; someone who studied and taught with the kind of objectivity that is unique to those of a noble spirit, to those who love the subject matter more than their subjectively selective curiosity. He had the courage for clarity where clarity was possible and also the courage for mystery. He could differentiate in order to unify. He could muster the fortitude to oppose common opinion without seeking attention or making novelty a criterion for truth, and, when it was necessary and no better solution could be found, he was even able to adhere to traditional opinion, though he may have sensed its lack of clarity and insufficiency.

In his theology, he talked about God and not about himself. He used prose, even though he could write poetry. He made careful calculations and still was willing to trade Paris for Chrysostom's "Commentary on the Gospel of Matthew." Even as a mature theologian, he was still able to learn new things and change his opinions. He always thought from the perspective of the whole and still had (as far as this is possible for a single individual) empathy for and concern with exploring the single issue. He spoke his mind without wishing to argue or assuming that his opponents were ignorant. One rarely hears of him having used a harsh word. He was magnificent in his theology not because he was the only and fully comprehensive theologian (an impossibility anyhow) or because he considered himself great, but because he thought "*in medio Ecclesiae*" ("from the center of the church") and remained open to anything that people of the past and of his own time were concerned with.

A priest in training has to be a theologian. He is not to be a schoolboy who manages to pass the exams only because it is a requirement for ordination. We need not be theological geniuses. But we have to be people and Christians who love theological insight and are engaged in its pursuit with our whole heart and mind. In the long run, we cannot have a truly spiritual life without a life of the mind. Theology requires that we allow God's word to take us over completely for everything we are, mind and spirit, for the entire weight and difficulty of our present life, for our entire life experience. Theology is not just what is written in theology books; theology is preparation for subsequent proclamation by the person as a whole, as a priest, into which flows and where is processed also what concerns or should concern the educated person of the time into which God has placed him without asking. That is how Thomas did it and that is how we should, too. If the living God has spoken to us and theology is nothing but a close listening for the revelation of God that employs every means of grace and nature available to humans, then we are to be theologians; otherwise, we are not anything much of what we should be. Theology is a part of us, an internal event of salvific proportions in our own lives and in those of others. It is certainly not a matter of being in school.

Thomas Was a Mystic

In saying that Thomas was a mystic we do not mean that Thomas was given to ecstasies, that he was a person who had extraordinary visionary experiences, someone who in the style of Spanish mysticism was concerned with his own subjective experiences in an almost introverted way. Of that one finds little or next to nothing in his writings. But he was a mystic insofar as he knew about the *latens Deitas*, the hidden God: *adoro te devote, latens Deitas* ("I adore you devoutly, Hidden God.") He knew of the hidden God of true silence, of the God beyond all that even most sacred theology is able to say of him, of the God who is loved as the one beyond comprehension. He knew of such a God not only in theory but also in the experience of his own heart, so much so that this experience had him fall silent and drop his writing tool in the end (*"suspendit organa scriptionis"*) with the words: *"paleae sunt, quae scripsi, frater Reginalede"* ("Everything I have written, Father Reginalede, is straw"). In the end, he left behind his life's home that had been lit by theology and escaped into the boundless vastness of God, "even though it was dark there." He stammered a little of the Song of Songs about love and then fell silent. This he did in order to let only God speak, the God in whose presence even the human words God himself used with us are but shadow and allegory. How true and fitting that this should have come only at the end of Thomas's life and that it actually did. This is as it should have been. What is to come at the end and only then has to have been implanted from the beginning as a hidden core in that hull which is the only place where it can ripen: in the monastic renunciation of life and in the struggle of theology for the light of God, the struggle for the light that is rewarded by the crucifying and blessed experience of the divine night, which is the only way by which the eternal light can rise.

As far as we are concerned, however, we are not there yet. Consequently, we should not pose in this final posture of the mature saint. Rather, we should practice in our lives to attain to this final experience, where people fall silent and turn off all lights in order to allow God to speak and allow his light alone to shine. We should practice this. When we live in dark times, when theology is laborious and its fruit seems only sparse, when faith has to continuously wrestle with great effort the deeply concealed disbelief of the mind and the heart, when illusion has to experience repeated disillusionment, when we have done everything and still remain unprofitable servants, when all invigorating strength is only the beginning of agony—as was the case for the Son of Man in the garden, when all enthusiasm is transformed into the tiresome duty of everyday life, then we are walking straight toward that hour when we, while carrying in our hands only the empty straw of our life and of our factual knowledge, will obtain as beggars the riches of eternity, riches that are truly and actually God himself. We are engaged in this practice when we are monks and theologians, like Thomas, happy people in our honest renunciation and thirsty listeners for the word of God.

Thomas is alive. He may seem far away to us. But he is not, because the communion of saints is near and the apparent distance is only an illusion. The saints may appear to us as if they had been extinguished by the blinding splendor of the eternal God into which they have entered, as if they had vanished into the distance of buried centuries. But time ripens into eternity, and God is not a God of the dead but of the living. Whatever has gone home to him is alive. And therefore Thomas is alive. We are asked whether our faith is alive enough, so that from among the thousands upon thousands of saints, Thomas, too, can play a part in our life.

IGNATIUS OF LOYOLA:
THE SAINT'S RELEVANCE FOR TODAY

The history of interpreting the relevance of a historical figure is never finished. Each generation has to discover anew what a leading role model in history may have to say. This simple fact provides an objective reason for the subjective choice of Ignatius of Loyola and this present reflection on him.

Ignatius was a sober man. He could afford this sobriety since he was already aglow from within and had no need to be "fired up" by sensational and impressive externals. He knew too much of the incomprehensibility of "divine majesty" to view uncritically the relativity of all earthly things, even in the loftier regions of the spiritual and the mystical life. What is called his rationalism, his almost technical inclination, originates from his relationship with God at its deepest source: God is so big that everything else besides him, even what stands in God's holy radius without being God himself, becomes strangely small; but precisely on account of the definite, unique majesty of a God who cannot be confused with anything else, the small also is to be valued for what it is. It can and has to be taken seriously for its own worth: for the creature can serve God only through creaturely means and its own insignificance does not relieve the creature of offering up to God at least this insignificance. That is why Ignatius appeared sober, laboring "as long as it is day" (Jn 9:4). That is why he was free of the fanaticism of a single method and of a single panacea. That is why he could adapt without losing his center. That is why he did not have the desire to look like a genius. That is why he was matter-of-fact and unswerving. It is why he hated big words and lofty programs. It is why he could labor without having to aim for concrete results. It is why he could use worldly means without becoming dependent on them, engaging human idiosyncrasies and even weaknesses without cynically despising people for them. It is why he could become quiet and disappear completely behind his task. It is why he died quietly, without even having received the sacraments of the church. He desired them but could not see his dying as important enough to make a fuss over a personal wish. In his holy sobriety before God, Ignatius considered as unimportant all things apart from the God he clearly discerned, and then those things became important again in a completely new way, namely from God's perspective.

Ignatius was an apostolic person. As much as he experienced the inexpressible majesty of God above all other existing

and imagined things, so much did he consider God and his
Christ as active in the world, as creative, as experiencing their
own story in the world, as still building their eternal kingdom,
as still having to come into "their own glory." For Ignatius,
God was not only the goal but also the innermost center of the
ongoing movement toward that goal.

Ignatius knew himself to be drawn toward the historical
movement of eternal love aimed at its own victory: he was
apostolic, or "sent." His concern was the care of souls. He
knew as his own sacred fulfillment only the honor of God and
the salvation of all for whom his beloved Lord died the death
of the cross and of desertion. For that reason, he had "to help
souls." And even in that regard, he was the saintly and sober
one. He worked as a faithful servant. He did not get intoxi-
cated by his own successes. He was not surprised by the fact
that the kingdom of God is always as if at death's door. He
knew from the start that the apostolate is always a labor along
with the Lord, who by his cross, hence by his own failure,
comes out victorious. Ignatius served the church by his mystical love for Christ's body in a way that few great people in
the kingdom of God have been graced to do. He was a mystic of the papacy who by his mysticism ushered in a new era
of the church. And yet, even in that he was modest and sober.
He saw the church as damaged and could endure looking at it
without covering up the pain through cheap enthusiasm or
bitterness. When he was told in a heavenly vision that God
would favor him in Rome, he interpreted this favor to possibly mean his crucifixion in Rome. When sick unto death, he
sent for the blessing of the Carafa Pope Paul IV, even though
he admitted that when it became known that this former opponent of his had been elected pope, all the bones in his body
were trembling.

His apostolate stands at the beginning of an era where the
faith had split the church, the place that for a thousand years
had been taken for granted to be there for everybody and for
everything, and had turned it into a church of the diaspora and

of the individual. Ignatius tried rightfully to stem this development and his efforts produced the success that we call the
church of the Catholic restoration and of the Baroque era. And
yet, he can also be called the true patron saint of the apostolate
in that age of world and church history at whose threshold we
currently stand. While his inspiration has produced people
who make decisions and carry them out on the soil of Holy
Mother church, the hierarchical church, that same inspiration
has also produced people who are able to remain "individualists" because they need to be. By "individualists" we do not
mean here the interpretation of the nineteenth century, referring to people who reap advantages from their individual traits,
consider them a right or an entitlement, and take pleasure in
seeing themselves as those who are singularly unique. Rather,
"individualists" are those willing to live with themselves and
their limitations without fleeing into the communal life or becoming disconsolate. They are people who have the courage to
meet their God in solitude, as in the individual *Exercises*, for example (which Ignatius never saw as a group exercise), by hearing and accepting God's thoroughly individualized call, even if
this call should lead to the foolishness of the cross, would not
find the ready approval of everyone, and could not be exclusively derived from general, rational-sounding principles. They
are people who occasionally can be left to their own devices so
that "the creator [can] deal with his creature and the creature
[can] deal with his or her creator and Lord in an immediate
fashion."

In light of these considerations, one may be allowed to say
that the time of Ignatius has yet to come and that the uniqueness of his apostolic endeavors has yet to be fully revealed.
From the very small arena of his apostolate, from Rome, Ignatius wrote that the "kingdom of the world is poor in good
fruit and overgrown with bad." This certainly is the signature
trait of our own time, hence the requirement that the church's
mission be carried out for a yet indefinite amount of time.
Therefore, it is precisely the people certain of their goals and

able to endure an immediate solitude with their God amidst a hostile world, which they accept as God's grace with a salvific purpose, who can live out an apostolate in the spirit of St. Ignatius and are called upon to help shape it in others—even and especially in our own day.

Ignatius is a loving person. He loves God. One could say that this is something to be taken for granted, especially in a saint. But not only is what is to be taken for granted and most ordinary also an ever new mystery and wonder, it is a strange and touching characteristic in a man who, while knowing so much of the inexpressible majesty and distance of God, could deal with his God in such an intimate, loving, and childlike way. He is near God and God is near him. He only has to open the gates of his soul and immediately he finds his God in the unshakeable knowledge that in this nameless silence and vastness, in this silence devoid of words and of the sound of individual objects, there is God and he alone, drawing the soul completely into his love. Ignatius once wrote: "Never forget that the Lord God loves you. Of that I have no doubt. Reciprocate with an equal love."

And since Ignatius is a lover of God, he can say in the same way as did Augustine before him: "In the Lord, you are permitted everything—apart from obvious mortal sins and with the exception of what you might consider as such—if you think it useful, if thereby your soul can gain considerable assistance and is more strongly compelled to love its creator and Lord!" Such love is modest, accepting of the way one is, and it knows: "Only after this life of our earthly misery are people set free from their ailments because God our creator and Lord will then completely burn away all our malice in the fiery flame of his eternal love."

The great saints in the kingdom of God have a mission that never quite vanishes once it has emerged from the hidden storehouse of the church's graces and has come to the attention of world history. After all, the church (even less so than a person) is not a creature that has to give up its own past in

order to have a future. If this is true of all great people and
events in the holy history of the church, then it is also and especially true of Ignatius. He is alive. His spirit is still alive and
he has a mission for the church of the future. It is possible that
only later church generations will recognize in him the arche-
typical and original, and thus the highly relevant role model
for the Christian of the immediate future. When we have the
feeling that before us still lies a dark and hidden future and are
wondering what a human being and a Christian will need to
look like in order to be a witness for God, for his grace and his
kingdom, we are likely to wish for a person with the very traits
that are presently drawing us to this saint.

THE MYSTICISM OF LOVING ALL THINGS
IN THE WORLD ACCORDING TO IGNATIUS

What is mysticism and what is the love of all things in the
world ("*Weltfreudigkeit*") and to what degree are they
both present in Ignatius of Loyola, so that one can speak of an
Ignatian mysticism that loves all things in the world? These
are apparently the questions raised by the title of this meditation, and it may well appear as if the question is aimed at
something that is not only hidden in the dark but contains a
contradiction in terms.

For what do the love of all things in the world and mysticism have in common? Does mysticism not refer to God and
a love of all things to the world? And what is the relationship
in Christian mysticism between God and the world, since for
Christians the world lies in shambles and they have heard the
voice of God about the free, transcendent revelation that calls
people out of the world into the life of the God who is beyond
this world? Is it not true for Ignatius as for any mystic what the
"first Ignatius," the apostle Paul, said: "The boundaries and
kingdoms of this world are of little avail to me; better by far to

die with Christ Jesus than to rule to the very corners of the earth"? Is not every type of mysticism a leaving of this life's and this world's home and an entering into the night of the senses and the spirit, so that when everything is quiet and the world's stars are dimmed, when one is crucified with Christ and all created things are dissolving and one is deserted, it is possible for one to perceive that which is uncreated? So, once again, what do mysticism and the love of all things in the world have in common?

This is not meant as a harmless theoretical question, one in which the question disappears as soon as the answer is given and explained. Rather, it is a question that can be correctly answered only when the question is properly informed by the answer. On the surface, the question seems to assume that we know what the love of all things in the world is. In reality, however, only the answer can tell us what is meant by the love of all things in the world in Ignatian mysticism. Certainly, we may associate with the phrase one or another thing, perhaps something great and important. But how do we know that we understand by the love of all things in the world that which the mystic means by it? It should be immediately clear that not just any way of being oriented to the world, of affirming the world, of rejoicing in the world or however one may call a readiness to enter the world and its beauty and challenge in a loving and engaged way, that not just any possible way of such an affirming attitude toward the world can be the way of the mystic. What, then, is the love of all things in the world for the mystic and for Ignatius in particular?

This much should be clear from our simple reflection: In regard to the question raised, we cannot merely import and presuppose a definition of the love of all things in the world in order to see now whether such a definition, which is ours, can be also found in Ignatius. With such an approach, we could certainly patch together this or the other thing we have read in the life and teachings of Ignatius. But it is questionable that this method would allow us to find the internal law of his life, the original spirit of his teachings. I am afraid that in the end we would be discovering only our own spirit while calling into question his. The only path accessible to us then is this: to ask about the mysticism of Ignatius first and then to proceed toward an understanding of what could be generally meant by the Ignatian and hence a Jesuit love of all things in the world.

The Mysticism of Ignatius

There are words in which are gathered the knowledge, the hope and love, the ideals of entire generations and centuries, words that want to say at once everything that touches people; and because they want to say everything, they are ever in danger of meaning everything, hence, nothing. In the history of Western thought, such words used to be *logos*, *enlightenment*, *spirit*, and *nation*, for example, along with others. To these words also belongs the word *mysticism*. This word is one of those by which people tried to describe everything they believed and wished existed. The word has a certain meaning to the poet of the Upanishads and to Lao Tzu, to Plotinus and to the Sufi sage, to Gregory of Nyssa, to Paracelsus, and to Goethe. But what is the meaning of the word when it is to have meaning to all of them?

We can say only what this word means to the Christian. For the Christian, mysticism means the experience of an immediate interaction between the personal God and the human being, an interaction that is grounded in Christ's grace. We do not want to say: *cognitio Dei experimentalis*, since at the least and to a considerable degree, mysticism goes beyond the mere *knowledge* of God or what is meant by that word today. Also, we do not want to say: experience of union with God, since we are then establishing a definition of mysticism that would contradict the distinction commonly made today in the history of religion between prophetic and mystical piety. Wherever the living God of Jesus Christ is acting upon the soul in an immediate way (which does not necessarily have to be a *visio beatifica* in the theological sense), there we have Christian mysticism. Such a loose definition of Christian mysticism will suffice for our present purpose.

Ignatius was truly a mystic. There can be no doubt about it. We will have to be satisfied with this assessment, even though we do not know any historical facts about his mysticism. While we cannot compare the knowledge we have of the interior lives of the great Spanish mystics Teresa of Avila and John of the Cross with that of Ignatius, what we do know of the mystical, grace-filled life of St. Ignatius is still significant. A detailed analysis of his book on the *Exercises*, his autobiography, his diary fragments, the reports of his intimate companions, such as Laínez, Nadal, and Polcano, actually afford us a rather clear picture of his mysticism. But we do not want to report here on his *pati divina* ("holy suffering"), as he himself calls it. Neither do we want to report on his mysticism regarding Jesus and the cross, his priestly liturgical mysticism, his Trinitarian mysticism; nor do we want to address the story of his mystical path, from the first visions at Manresa, his "first church," as he calls this, to the time in upper Italy which climaxed in the vision of La Storta, up to his time in Rome, the time of his mystical perfection, where beyond all visions he was always with his God, so that Laínez, the great theologian and his confidant, could say about him: *visiones omnes tum reales . . . tum per species et repraesentationes iam transgressus versatur nunc in pure intellectualibus, in unitate Dei.* Those who have some familiarity with the theory of Catholic mysticism can at least vaguely make out what these simple words of Laínez suggest with regard to the long ascents of this mystic, until he entered into the simple, lit darkness of God: *in unitatem Dei.*

But all of this should not be the point of discussion here. For we need address Ignatius's mysticism only to the degree that it clarifies what is actually meant by it and what uniquely defines an Ignatian love of all things in the world. When we try to understand his mysticism from this perspective, it is clear that what is important is not the specific nature of his mystical piety or how his piety differs from that of a common piety and a "normal" life of prayer, which does not have the same intensity and degree of immediacy with God that the mystic experiences in his or her relationship with God. As long as we are aware that the nature of one's piety lends it a unique depth and power, it is proper to simply ask about the nature of Ignatian piety, from which one can clarify the reason for and meaning of his love of all things in the world.

When trying to interpret Ignatian piety from this perspective, it appears that two observations can be made:

1. Ignatian piety is a piety of the cross; in that can be seen its essential continuity with the overall current of an earlier Christian piety and its Christian nature.

2. Because Ignatian piety is Christian, it is a piety directed at the God who is beyond this world. Such an emphasis mainly constitutes this piety's uniqueness and the most fundamental reason for and meaning of its love for all things in the world.

One will first have to say something about each of these statements.

1. Ignatian piety is a piety of the cross as was all earlier Christian mystical piety. To overlook this basic feature would be to completely misunderstand Ignatian piety. We have to acknowledge first and foremost that Ignatian piety is and wants to be a "monastic" piety. By "monastic" is not meant the canonical regulations or the external form through which members live in community. Rather, "monastic" is to be understood in its theological and metaphysical sense, in terms of the word's basic and ultimate meaning. By that we mean to say that Ignatius consciously and clearly adopts and continues in his life, in his piety, and in the spirit he bestows upon his order this ultimate orientation of life from which Catholic monasticism, the "*monazein*," originally resulted and from which it continues to draw its existence. Proof of this is the simple fact

that he and his followers took the vows of poverty, celibacy, and obedience. By doing so, they explicitly adopted the attitude of the *monachos*, the solitary, who by his distance from the world is alone in God. Ignatius is one of those people who by a *fuga saeculi* (a "flight from this age") flee with their whole being into the desert, even though it is the secular stone desert of the big city, in order to look for God far away from the world. It is nothing but superficiality when one allows the difference of the external way of life to cover up the deepest and most fundamental commonality of the Jesuit and the monk that governs the ideal of all Catholic monastic life.

But what is the monk? He is a man who has put on the mantle of Christ. He is a man who by his asceticism, of which poverty and virginity are paradigms, tries and ideally tries again to allow the existential and fundamental dying with Christ in baptism to become a living reality in its fullest meaning throughout his entire life. In the early church, Christian perfection and martyrdom were almost identical, so that the martyrs represented the first order of saints, still called "confessors" today, and that next to them in the ecclesiastical categories of saints there actually existed only the category of virgin, since their nature, too, is nothing but the martyrdom of the invisible, silent struggle and dying within one's self. This spirit of the early church is what the monk seeks to carry on, while the empirical question about the connection between persecution and monasticism can be put aside here. Thus, the monk is the one who dies in Christ. He takes upon himself the renunciation the Lord took on, is clothed in his robe, is poor for Christ's sake, is the person for whom is submerged the enjoyment of the world by the practice of poverty, the enjoyment of earthly love by virginity, the enjoyment of the secret pleasure of self-determination by renouncing his own will for the sake of another's; he is still the one who prays the early Christian prayer: "May grace come and the world depart" (*Didache*, 10). To use a mystical expression, the monk flees from the light of this world into the night of the senses and of the spirit in order to receive the grace and the mercy of the eternal God.

Did Ignatius have in mind any other type of life, or did he choose another? He wants to follow the poor Jesus, the despised one, the ridiculed one, the crucified one. The height he wants us to reach by the *Exercises* is the foolishness of the cross. "Lovingly," says Ignatius, "are we to direct the spirit toward it—for this is most important and decisive to our creator and Lord—and to see how much all growth in the spiritual life depends on renouncing completely and not just halfway all that the world loves and longs for, and to accept with one's whole soul, even to demand, what Christ our Lord has loved and taken upon himself...For those who walk like that in the spirit and in the true discipleship of Christ the Lord have only one love and one burning desire: to wear the Lord's robe and his mark out of love and respect for him. If doing so does not insult the divine majesty and cause sin in one's neighbor, they desire on their own accord the pain of disgrace and insult and injustice, a treatment and status granted only to fools. And all of that simply because they have only one desire: imitating and following Jesus Christ, their creator and Lord, in his robe and with his mark, which he has worn for the sake of our salvation as an example to us, so that we might imitate him and follow him with all our strength enabled by his grace, the one who is the true way that introduces people to life" (*Constitutiones*, "Examen generale," 4, 44).

Is such an attitude the love of all things in the world and an affirmation of the world? However one may ultimately answer this question, this much is certain: Ignatius does not wish to affirm for himself and his followers the type of love of all things in the world in which the world and God, time and eternity are from the outset reconciled into a blissful harmony. This means that Ignatius's love of all things in the world is not the kind by which people are primarily those who are in the world, that is, those who accept the world's goodness and its challenge as their primary responsibility in order to strive to fulfill their internal human nature and finally and possibly much, much later expect their blessedness with God—a blessedness that one assumes to be guaranteed only when one has met a few requirements of a certain judicial and ritualistic nature, apart from meeting the ordinary demands of the world and leading a moral life.

Did we not slip into the opposite of where we wanted to be now, into the *fuga saeculi*, rather than the love of all things in the world? The answer to this question will become also the path that leads us to the nature and meaning of Ignatius's love of all things in the world. And both are grounded in what we have called the second basic statement about Ignatian piety.

2. Ignatian piety is a piety directed at the God who freely reveals himself as far beyond this world. To say it again: This fact is the reason for the flight from the world and contains in it the possibility of embracing the world.

In order to grasp this characteristic of Ignatian piety, we will first try to consider it from the perspective we have assumed so far. Hence we ask: What is the ultimate reason for the Christian flight from the world that has come to be expressed in monasticism and in Ignatian piety as a piety of the cross?

In Christianity, hence in Jesus Christ, the living and personal God has addressed the person. A terrifying fact has thus entered human life, a fact that precludes the possibility that human existence can be a self-enclosed, internal harmony with God. Certainly, it is possible to discern God in his creation and in the world. But such recognition is uniquely ambiguous.

On the one hand, we recognize God as the origin of the world, as the one ensuring its life, as the ultimate ground of human and the world's existence. Thus, we recognize God to the degree that he reveals himself in the mirror of the world, so that it almost looks as if the world were the aim of God, at least of the kind of God who when he does reveal himself to us in the world is the one we encounter only as philosophers.

On the other hand, we also recognize in the quest for God in metaphysics the God who is both the ground of the world, with the world as God's aim, and the free, personal, infinite God who is the God beyond all the world's finitude, so that the world cannot actually reveal what this God is and can be, namely, one who is personal and free and infinite. The world cannot show us the aim of God. With that, human metaphysics with its quest for God reaches its end and shows its chief failure: In its quest for God, metaphysics is confronted with a free, self-contained person, with a God who may choose to remain silent, the *theos sigon*, as Origen once called him. And what this infinite God is in himself and how this free, personal God wishes to deal with us, this dark and yet crucial question that governs our life, cannot be answered through the light of reason. Whether he wants to meets us in an immediate and personal way, whether he wants to remain silent, what he wants to say to us in case he desires to speak, all of that remains to metaphysics—to all thought that starts with the world and with human longing in an attempt to know—a basic mystery. Hence, all metaphysics would have to end up in the ever-conscious readiness of people to listen for what lies beyond them in order to determine whether this distant, silent Someone might wish to say something, end up in a readiness for the faintest possibility of a revelation.

But are people able to endure such an *ex-stasis* in their lives, able to endure such a waiting for God? Are they not always tempted to view the world as the final revelation of God, thereby making God the aim of the world and the world the aim of God? Apart from Christianity, was there ever in human history a philosophy—beginning with the Greeks and continuing through to Hegel—that did not succumb to this temptation? In all philosophy, was God not ultimately the *anima mundi*, the God who can exist in the world only as the world's own transfiguration, as the world's secret gleam of the absolute? And is this ongoing sin in the history of philosophy and in the area of knowing not an expression of what repeatedly happens in the life of the unsaved: to permit God to be only what the world is, to create God in the image of the human being, to conceive of piety as a devotion to the world?

All idolatry is nothing but the concrete expression of the existential attitude of people that builds upon the belief that God is nothing more than the original unity of all powers that permeate this world and human destiny. Even Hegel's spiritual philosophy still prays to an idol: to the absolute spirit that comes into its own in humans and in their development of self. A God after our own hearts, after our own image and reflection, would be a God with nothing else to do but to permit people to grow and multiply, blessing them in their activity of subduing the earth; he would be nothing more than what we can positively make out about him, hence, nothing more than the ever faraway horizon in which the finite human infinity unfolds according to human laws, nothing but the divinity of the world. And it then makes little difference whether this God, created in our image, bears the characteristics of Apollo or Dionysus.

But God is more than that. And as the one who is more than the world, God has broken into human existence and has burst apart this world and what theology calls "nature." He has revealed himself in Jesus Christ. This revelation has happened in the dual unity of supernatural existence and of the word. The ultimate aim of this revelation is to call people out of the world into the life of God, who is leading his personal life in inaccessible light as the one who is above all the world, as the God in three persons. God thus concretely confronts people with a demand and a call catapulting them off the track that is previously prescribed by their human nature and lodged within the world's range of vision. A transcendence of the former task and destiny of humans is thereby created, a transcendence that gives the inevitable impression of being in contradiction with nature and the world, both of which are always innately disposed to form a closed unit and are tempted to strive for completion by their own powers, even where God is considered to form the ultimate origin and backdrop. Everything called "nature" is the finite that does not result from an immediate encounter with the free God who reveals himself by speech, and this nature as the self-enclosed and intrinsically whole is always inclined to come to rest within itself, to maintain harmony within its own current system and to perfect it. When God then confronts nature in a revelatory way, there is the highly concrete possibility that he might give humans commands that are no longer the voice or the law of nature (*lex naturae*). And when God calls people by this command of his revelatory word to a supernatural, otherworldly life, as has actually happened in the revelation of Christ, then this command is always and by necessity a breaking open of the self-enclosed nature in which the world wants to come to rest, hence a demotion whereby the world—even a good world, when measured by the standards of God's will and laws—becomes preliminary, a thing of second rank subject to a standard no longer its own.

Thereby is also made possible a sacrificing of the world, a renunciation, a flight from the world, a releasing of the world's goods and values that goes beyond what would appear reasonable, provided that these goods and values constitute in the natural order the highest fulfillment for the task that human existence demands. Such a flight from the world is not only meaningful but even and in some sense necessary. The darkness of the Christian faith is its fundamental and decisive beginning. Such a flight from the world becomes necessary because when one has to anticipate the possible, free, revelatory activity of the personal God (which is one of the basic tenets of the finite mind in any hypothesis), the actual occurrence of such a revelation leads inexorably to the duty to live out practically the need to obey the God of revelation. Apart from the unreserved acceptance of such a revealed message about the supernatural life, the only conceivable human response to the God of revelation calling from beyond the world is a sacrifice of the world that goes beyond a reasonable internal and divinely guided ethic, for people can profess only by their lives that God has transported the center of their human existence outside the world by concretely replacing their worldly existence with that of a *fuga saeculi*. Thus, all Christian dying has already fundamentally superseded the warring efforts of self-control that pertain to a pure ethic—without necessarily excluding the latter, of course—and has always been, as the early Christian *Didache* says in its prayers, an allowing of the world to pass by so that grace may come. Christianity is essentially a *fuga saeculi* because it is a profession of the personal God of grace freely revealed in Christ, a grace that is not the fulfillment of the immediate longing of the world for its completion, even though in the end times it will bring about in a superior way this world's perfection. Professing the cross, which unites monastic and Ignatian piety, is only a concrete realization of the intrinsically Christian flight from the world.

It may appear that with these considerations we have strayed from our topic. But that is not the case, for by such a theological metaphysics, which identifies the profession of the cross as the first and basic characteristic of Ignatian piety, we have already prepared ourselves for the meaning of the second basic characteristic.

The God of Ignatian piety is the God of supernatural grace who freely and personally deals with people in a "historical" manner. There can be no doubt about this. In Ignatian piety, God is *divina maiestas*, the Lord on whose sovereign will everything depends, before whom it is not people with their longing and will that count but only what his divine majesty desires. Since this God is the freely acting one above all the world, Ignatius is mostly concerned with how this God has historically dealt with people, for only God's free deed in history can reveal to us what he himself is like and how he desires to be in relationship with people. The contemplation of the angels' fall, original sin, and the life of Jesus in the *Exercises* has its ultimate rationale in such a view of God. If the *Exercises* are a singular, great asking for the most holy will of his divine majesty, then this will is not meant to be like the one manifest in the will and longing of one's own heart; the search is for the will of this free God by which God still freely governs human judgment, human will, and the human heart. All discernment of the spirits, this important piece of the *Exercises*, has its ultimate rationale in the fact that, in the final analysis, it is not a discernment of the longings in one's own heart based on common moral standards, but a listening for the commanding word of God, a searching and finding of the free command of the personal God aimed at the will of the person in his or her own concrete circumstances. And since this God meets Ignatius in Jesus Christ, Ignatius confesses to the cross and to the foolishness of Christ's way. For all this foolishness of the cross is to him only the expression and practice of the willingness to follow this free God, even when he calls one out of the world, away from its own meaning and its light into the light of God where people feel they are entering the night.

But precisely this attitude, resulting from such a view of God and the willingness to accept the cross, produces the Ignatian affirmation of the world and the love of all things in the world. And now, having clarified at least in its broadest outline the basic characteristics of Ignatian piety and mysticism, we are able to understand the meaning and nature of the Ignatian affirmation of the world.

The Love of All Things in the World in Ignatius

In order to arrive at the meaning of such a love of all things in the world, we have to begin yet once more with the general theological meaning of the Christian flight from the world. The *fuga saeculi*, which essentially belongs to the Christian life, appeared to us as the profession of God as far as God, being beyond the world, constitutes our inner center and the aim of our Christian life; it is an existential enacting of the already completed displacement of the center of our existence into the triune God that has been made possible by the revealed God of grace. But this existential profession can be authentic only when it truly professes the God of free grace. This means that for this profession to truly affirm the center of our life as one that lies beyond this world, it also has to profess that this new center of our life has been granted to us solely by the freely given grace of God, not on account of a sacrificial flight from the world.

Thus one can see that the Christian flight from the world differs from a worldly yet divinely inspired ethic with its demands for renunciation, provided this ethic were truly a flight from the world and not merely an attempt to control the world and one's self. But the Christian *fuga saeculi* differs also from the non-Christian negation of the world found in orphic, neo-Platonist, and Buddhist asceticism and mysticism. For all these expressions of a flight from the world ultimately start with the human being and from below, so to speak, and they all equally consider renunciation and becoming nothing as the instrument that of its own accord and all by itself can forcibly produce an awareness of the absolute. All such attempts at becoming nothing may be aimed at opposing the direct divinizing of the world, but in reality they are only its parallel path. To such non-Christian forms of mysticism, renunciation and the flight from the world are already the attaining of God. By contrast, Christianity acknowledges the free grace of God, which means a divine life in humans that depends first and foremost on the free, personal, and loving activity of God. Therefore, Christianity knows that dying, renunciation, and flight from the world cannot on their own generate the possession of the absolute, that such asceticism is not the path by which humans can force their way into gaining access to the interior life of God. Christians know that their flight from the world is only the response and necessary gesture toward the God who freely reveals and discloses himself and who gives himself to us in freely given love.

If in this sense God's grace is free, then Christians know, despite their exceeding love for the foolishness of the cross, that the free God will bless even those human works (and transform them from his perspective into advancing steps) that do not yet bear the characteristic dying of a flight from the world, which gains meaning only when it is a dying into the new life of God. When people have surrendered to the demand of the self-revelatory God in faith even once, then God is able to accept by grace their service in the world, which is his world and creation after all, as the path to him who is beyond the world, so that people will not only encounter the absolute God as in radical contradiction to the world but also as in the world. Once people have placed themselves beneath the cross and have died with Christ, once they have entered the darkness of the faith and the ecstasy of love for the distant God, any one of their intrinsically good acts, to use the language of scholastic theology, even a truly worldly act, can be supernaturally elevated by grace, thereby transcending its worldly meaning in aim and nature beyond the *ordo legis naturae* and reaching into the life of God himself. This fact robs the Christian flight from the world of any hubris, which it could have if it were the exclusive path to God. In their flight from the world to God, Christians have to acknowledge also that even through the world one can attain to this God who is beyond this world from which Christians have detached themselves in order to find him. Those who are virgins for God's sake have to acknowledge that marriage is a sacrament; those who are living the *vita contemplativa* by fleeing from the world are doing so in a Christian way only when they are keenly aware that God has also blessed the *vita activa* of worldly responsibility and has made it a life that is godly.

These background considerations also generate the Ignatian affirmation of the world. That something like this truly exists has always been known, though it has been rarely understood in its true core. Adaptation, affirmation of the demands of a certain time period, cultivation of culture, love for the sciences, the incorporation of humanism and of the individualism of the Renaissance, the cheerful serenity of the Baroque, the avoidance of external forms of monasticism, all that and much more has rightfully come to be regarded as the Jesuit affirmation of the world. But one has truly understood this attitude only when one can explain it from its underlying spirit and the way this spirit, caught by those of the seventeenth and eighteenth centuries, compelled the followers of Ignatius to build Baroque churches with their cheerful exuberance of a bright, transfigured world and, at the same, compelled them to enlist for the faraway missions to end up dying painful deaths for Christ in the boiling springs of Japan and the bamboo cages of Tonking.

Ignatius moves from God to the world, not the other way around. Since he has surrendered in prayerful humility to the God beyond this world and to his will, Ignatius is prepared for the same reason to obey God's word, even when God pushes him out of the still desert he had sought during his daring flight toward God, when God pushes him back into the world, a world he had the courage to leave behind for the foolishness of the cross.

Thus a double characteristic emerges that is unique to the Ignatian love of all things in the world: the maxims of "*indiferencia*" and of "finding God in all things." The first is the prerequisite for the second.

By *indiferencia* is meant the willing readiness for any command of God, an equanimity resulting from the awareness that God is always greater than all we know of him, greater than that in which we can find him, and a repeated letting go of any specifics about the place in which we are inclined to imagine God meets us. Thus, the uniqueness of Ignatian piety lies less in the material, in the cultivation of a certain thought, in a special exercise, and in a unique way of finding God, than in the formal and ultimate attitude toward all thinking, exercises, and paths because one's possessing of God still has to allow God to be greater than all possessions. From such an attitude of *indiferencia* naturally results the ongoing readiness to hear a new call from God to tasks other than the present ones; to continually be willing to leave those areas in which one wanted to find and serve God. From it grows the willingness to be prepared like a servant for the sudden new command, aware of the duty to be transformed and to have no enduring place other than the place of restless change that is oriented toward the resting God; the courage not to consider one way to him as *the* way and to be open to looking for him on all paths. Such an attitude of *indiferencia* governs the passionate love of the cross, a love willing to be taken into the sorrow of Christ's death. It means a "yes" to the cross, provided his divine majesty may deign to call one to such a life unto death. *Indiferencia* is possible only with a lively will to a *fuga saeculi*, while conversely such an *indiferencia* also conceals this love of the foolishness of the cross by the common modesty of a normal, reasonable lifestyle. From such an *indiferencia*, Ignatius is able to do without expressions of mystical graces: God is present even beyond the world of mystical experiences. And Ignatius can do without the mystical gift of tears when his doctor orders it, whereas St. Francis upon facing the same objections and orders from his doctor angrily discarded them.

In short, such an *indiferencia* is a looking for God in all things. Since God is bigger than everything else, he can allow himself to be found in our flight from the world and he can also come to meet us in the streets of the world. And so Ignatius knows only one remedy for his ongoing restlessness regarding God: to look for him in all things, which also means looking for him always where he allows himself to be found, and it means also looking for him in the world if he wishes to show himself there. In such a looking for God in all things, we find the Ignatian formula for the higher synthesis of the two branches of piety that religious studies have commonly separated: the mystical as a flight from the world and the prophetic as a divinely ordained mission within the world. In the Ignatian formula, these opposites are in Hegel's words "reconciled." Ignatius is concerned only with the God who is beyond the world and who is not merely the dialectical antithesis of the world, with the God who allows himself to be found in the world whenever his sovereign will orders us to go there.

The Greek coloration of the terms aside, we find this dialectic between flight from the world and affirmation of the world also in the two medieval Christian terms of *contemplatio* and *actio*, the *vita contemplativa* and the *vita activa*. *Contemplatio* is the clinging to a God who is the aim of the Christian life, hence the God of a supernatural life. *Actio* is the fulfillment of the worldly task, including the natural and moral one. From this tentative definition of these terms, we can understand the formula of the Ignatian affirmation of the world, which originated within the first circle of his followers: *in actione contemplativus*. Ignatius was looking only for the God of Jesus Christ, the free, personal, absolute one: *contemplativus*. He knew that he could also look for him and find him in the world if God should desire it: *in actione*. And so Ignatius was willing with an attitude of *indiferencia* to look for him and for him alone, only for him, but for him also everywhere, also in the world: *in actione contemplativus*.

We will have to stop here. We have not been able to touch on many other questions, either those resulting from a need for more detailed interpretation or new questions that may have been raised on the basis of what was said. For example, we did not touch upon how the basic Ignatian attitude is specifically shaped by its intentional apostolate in the church's service and mission. Neither did we address how this Ignatian attitude, which is first that of the monk and member of a religious order, would look like when transposed to the level of a concrete lay piety.

During a time of bloody persecutions and after having been made to flee from his place of influence, Clement of Alexandria wrote his "miscellanies" at the beginning of the third century. In the midst of destruction and ruin, he formulated in his seventh book the wonderful thought that the perfect Christian would have to be the Christian who was *kosmios kai hyperkosmios*, both worldly and otherworldly at once. This thought can be an exhortation concerning our own attitude today: We are Christians, which means we live from the God

who is beyond this world and we live into him. In him is the
center of our Christian life. And so this life cannot be shaken,
even if it looks as if dark clouds are forming over the land of
the Occident. The cross of Christ belongs to our Christian life
and when it truly meets us in daily life, in the fate of our nation, when the hour of darkness seems to have arrived, it is to
us Christians not the failure of our life but the sadness that
comes with having no lasting home here and not wanting to
because one is on the way to a God who is beyond all worldly
fulfillment, is *hypercosmios*. And yet, in Clement's words, we are
to be *cosmios*: from the strength that places us above the world
we enter the world and its task, sent by the one with whom we
are one in the mystical life. *Kosmios kai hypercosmios.*

This is the attitude that Ignatian piety and mysticism
teach us. The Ignatian affirmation of the world is not a naïve
optimism, not a putting ourselves up in the world as if we had
in it the center of our life. The Ignatian love of all things in
the world grows out of the mysticism that is united to him
with whom we have become one in the foolishness of the
cross that flees this world. But once we have found the God
of life beyond, an attitude manifests itself in us that breaks
forth into the world from its deep seclusion in God, is active
as long as it is day, comes to fruition in the task of the present
hour of this world, and still waits with great longing for the
coming of the Lord.

MYSTERIES OF EVERYDAY LIFE

A LITTLE SONG

Many people today listen to music. We can get it from the radio like water from a faucet. The only thing we have to do is turn it on. But few people make music. Few sing. And even fewer can sing a new song from their heart. This is the case despite the fact that those wishing to be human can hardly do without such a song, just as they cannot do without play and dance. Such a song, when sung as one's own, can lead a person back to who he or she is and need not be "great music." Just as in addition to the great works of poetry, the arts, philosophy, and theology there are the wise sayings of everyday life, the good and well-meant adages that people can use to express themselves and by which they can find their way back to themselves and which even God acknowledges, there also has to be in addition to great music the "little song."

This song is important because little people (who also have eternal life ahead of them and hence are infinitely great) use it to tell who they are. There has to be a little song which, when heard once, can be sung or quietly whistled in everyday life, penetrating the mind and mood like an echo originating from the bottom of one's heart and telling of the self and of life's mystery, called God, what one's life is like in all its dimensions to keep from suffocating in one's own silence. And such a song has to exist also in those areas where people are most human and honest with themselves: where God meets them and where they meet God. It is the reason even the ancient sacred songs in church hymnals cannot substitute for the song that arises from the heart. These hymns are the necessary "tradition" that attest to the fact that before God people sing, that people have to acknowledge even in song that they have spiritual forebears who have passed on to others what is eternally young and fresh about God. But people also have a need to sing about themselves, about this ever new and unique person they are, each in their own way.

What deadly danger looms for us when nearly all new music written today is only great religious music (or the kind of music that wants to be great), music that is so solemn and official that one can sing it even in church, in the company of all during holy office, and—what terrible irony!—one does so only there? Is it not frightening that only few new compositions in religious music exist that allow one to feel that they are the songs of one's own "private" piety, the very piety by which one is to work out one's salvation in everyday life? Should there not be such music? One should be able to whistle it. It would not need to have more depth and profundity than everyday life, which is fully sufficient and already contains plenty. Or do religious things have a place only in the elevated moments of life? Does the Word become flesh lack the courage to live in the smallness of our ordinary moments?

One should invent such a new little song when in a good mood and when gratefully going off on vacation. Who, after all, thinks of humming: "All I do, I do for God" ("Alles meinem Gott zu Ehren")? We do not sing like that anymore, though one would hope that our song is still saying something to that effect. With the singing of such a little song, the heart's heaviness would lift. Or who, while doing the dishes, is really singing "O Sacred Heart, Surrounded"? Perhaps the rhythmic humming of the tires of a heavy truck could inspire a new sacred song. Why not? Or does true religion belong only to Sunday-like sentiments and to an elevated cultural consumerism for which the federal government foots the bill, since it would be too costly otherwise?

When listening to the French Jesuit Aimé Duval and uncertain as to whether one is allowed to listen and sing along in an unrestrained, simple, and plain manner and with a joyous heart, one should be pondering these and similar things.

And something else: It is rather cheap to quickly label and put down something in one's own mind and before others as "sentimental." In fact, one should not be afraid to feel sentimental. Fear is appropriate only for those who lack common sense. The others can afford to be "sentimental," which means they can entrust themselves to the original sentiment of their heart.

ABOUT SEEING AND HEARING

It appears that both seeing and hearing are basic to human experience. In order to say this, it is not necessary to ask the old question of how many "senses" humans have. "Tasting" may perhaps be regarded as a rudimentary form of seeing, because it is experienced only in connection with seeing and hearing, whereby one distinguishes between self and the other and thereby connects. Who has not noticed when eating or smoking in the dark that the sense of taste does not reach its fullest potential? But even those who doubt this fact might consider hearing and seeing as particularly concrete instances of original human experience and need not reject what follows as fundamentally flawed.

A popular "philosophy" of life will consider seeing and hearing as solely two gates through which the world and the environment step into our space of subjectivity, or as two bridges that carry us across the ditch of "subject" and "object." This popular view, derived as it is from Western antiquity, simply accepts these two gates and bridges as a fact, with the assumption that they could be also quite different—thus transmitting completely different experiences. Such a point of view will also say that other biological organisms apparently have a completely different world of the senses, that our senses leave out much of what is equally concrete around us, that our factually given senses have a coincidental, a-priori filter which, though biologically useful, pre-selects, thus preventing much from entering and refusing much from exiting: we do not see ultraviolet rays, we do not hear the acoustical waves that a bat can perceive with its sonar, we do not have an organ that registers radar, hence can approach vast areas of material reality only indirectly and with the assistance of interfacing instruments. In short, we view our capacity to see and hear as similar to that of a radio receiver that unfortunately cannot receive short wave, so that we seek consolation over the primitive build of our radios by saying that for the concrete necessities of life they are at least sufficient and that for such a purpose they are not built badly at all.

Still, such a "popular philosophy" of seeing and hearing appears a little primitive. First of all, without going into further detail here, a true metaphysics of humans cannot pattern the human sense organs on the model of mechanical tools such as, for example, a microscope that would be placed in front of our desire to see and would allow us to see only what its construction, independent from our desire to see, permits. We not only have sense organs, but we *are* our sensuality. Our physicality, hence our sensuality, comes from within and is built by the personal-spiritual subject itself; it is the way by which the spirit or the free subject, with its ongoing openness to the totality of all possible reality, deliberately enters the world. If this is the case, then it is not possible to say that the "glasses" of hearing and seeing, constituting our sense organs, have been put on us from the outside and could just as well have been different ones. Their biological "utility" can be understood only by recognizing that they are especially fit for us as spiritual beings living in the world, not only within our particular environment. For example, the nose of a dog is, from a biological viewpoint, useful in its "sensuality" for the dog's life. Hence, one can ask about the "usefulness" of our sense organs also. However bold such a thesis may sound, we might say that if such a spiritual disposition exists (not a sensuality that would be again defined by us) and builds its own "receiver," then this disposition wants to hear and see just as we, in fact, do. Seeing and hearing are the ways by which the spirit in the process of opening itself up allows for an immediate encounter. This encounter, which one sets out to experience and permits in the process of hearing and seeing, is intended for loving communication among physical beings in whom the spirit resides, so that in it the absolute mystery of God can speak.

Seeing and hearing on the one hand and intercommunication on the other imply by their unity and difference the problem that exists between the aesthetically and the morally religious, which, of course, cannot be addressed here in greater detail. Likewise, the argument regarding the origin of sensuality in the spirit, which shows itself as sensuous, cannot be explored further here. Of course, one could call such an argument ridiculous and caution about the possibility that one day on a distant planet there might be discovered physical, intelligent beings who communicate with their environment through completely different senses than seeing and hearing. One might argue that today's scientific knowledge of the world proves that the human spirit is striving to understand reality as a whole, while hearing and seeing only offer a tiny piece of it, so that the spirit from its end would have to laboriously find an indirect path toward this whole of reality and hence could be regarded as a physical spirit whose doors to the world had been open all along and continue to be. But let us maintain the original argument, and let us ask what it means when truly understood.

First of all, it is not the case that hearing and seeing offer only a small amount of starting material that is later processed by the (intelligent, scientific) mind, or human spirit, until it arrives at a newly self-constructed world, which is then viewed as the mirror image of the objective world, since essentially the former appears to come closest to the latter; one would thereby make "sensuous material" out to be a strange and ultimately amorphous intermediary substance between the objective world and that of the spirit. Since the spirit alone allows for the forming of sensuality (as Thomas Aquinas says) and retains this sensuality (*anima est forma corporis*), the spirit has arrived at its own perfection when it truly hears and sees, which means it does so in a spiritual sense, from its very basis, in its infinite horizon with all that it entails. Thereby, the spirit turns toward the image in what one might even call a "conversion," without which there is no true knowing, just as Thomas says in his doctrine about the "*Conversio ad phantasma*" or as does Kant, for whom true knowing is not possible without an image. Both the concrete image in its "light," conveyed by its colors to the one perceiving it, and the formed word with its horizon of understanding—both of these in the infinity into which they are placed—constitute the full happening of spirit.

What accompanies this image of seeing and of the word should not be confused with what is truly sought after by the spirit. On the one hand, there is the pure horizon of the infinite fullness of the spirit by which alone the image becomes concrete and perceivable, the infinity of the silent and sheltering mystery of holy silence. Wherever we see images or hear words as originating from this mystery, wherever we seek shelter in it and are able to conceive in these images or words the experience of the invisible and inexpressible mystery, we are dealing with fundamental or Ur-images (of nature or the arts), as in the case of the Apollo that Rilke considers in his poem, or we are dealing with fundamental or Ur-words. Nothing more lies behind these images because they are everything: in them, the infinite mystery is present. The poet Angelus Silesius says in *The Cherubinic Wanderer* (IV, 159):

"How did St. Benedict see the world in a piece of coal? In everything, there lies concealed and hidden all." Only by seeing (or hearing) in this manner are we truly seeing and hearing. The fact that we tend not to see or hear in this way but gauge things in a technical and utilitarian fashion and consider them items of active manipulation for the sake of everyday biological or scientific survival purposes does not take away from the truth but, rather, convicts us of lacking authenticity and is a sign of our fallen state. Today, we will have to re-learn with some difficulty the ability to genuinely hear and see. All true art of image and of word yearns to teach us that.

What is called "meditation on the image" in the religious sphere has its origin here. So does the teaching of the "spiritual senses" in its long Christian tradition and the exercise of "applying the senses" in the mystical contemplation of Ignatius of Loyola. Christians might also consider what is said in the first letter of John: "What we have heard, what we have seen with our eyes, what we have looked at and touched with our hands, concerning the word of life..." They should realize that the incarnation of the word of God and the fundamental or Ur-experience that John invokes here are destroyed in their essence when one assumes that seeing and hearing are only jumping-off points that one leaves behind in order to achieve a true understanding of an abstract, non-concrete, and wordless nature.

On the other hand, there is the scientific world of abstract terminology, which should not be scorned. It is part of human life and people have to enter this field, not only for the purposes of biological survival but also because it is where the spirit is active in the world. This field belongs to human activity also and people have to actualize themselves there beyond a mere contemplative relation to the world. However, when the liberal arts, such as philology and history, do not go back to seeing and hearing the concrete image, they become empty talk. When philosophy and theology contain no Ur-words, they cease to be true philosophy and theology and lose the story of the word that permits mystery to hold sway over us.

What about the natural sciences? They have certainly expanded our knowledge of and our power over things to an immense degree. But if their mathematically formulated statements about functional connections in the physical world are not to become pure mathematics and theoretical flights of fancy, they have to preserve the connection with immediate sense experience. What they need to say concretely, not merely mathematically, can be made clear only by means of things that are immediately heard and seen and by models that point ultimately to what we physically experience. The work of broadening the biological sphere and expanding theoretical knowledge through the natural sciences is ultimately at the service of the spirit revealed as absolute mystery in the world by our simple seeing and hearing of our environment and by the loving exchange between people. Thus, all sciences lead one back to this original, basic seeing and hearing of Ur-images by which people come to recognize the holy, sheltering mystery, especially when considering the fact that the Ur-image is people themselves, each of whom is, as image, the uniquely expressed word of this mystery's love.

Is there not a struggle between seeing and hearing? Did not the Greek/Western philosophical tradition almost entirely view people as those who see the "image" of existence, while the Christian tradition (beginning with the Old Testament and all the way through to Luther's view that only the ears are a Christian's sense organs) says that the word alone is powerfully spoken to us and brings into existence what it proclaims, thus generating as the basis of human existence the contradiction between a "submissive" hearing and a "take-charge" seeing? Is there not the complaint that people today no longer like to read, hence prefer hearing, and like only to look at pictures? It would be a foolish undertaking to try and settle the dispute between eyes and ears in an attempt to declare which of the two is more directly and radically linked with the origin of human existence. Those reading Jesus' words in the Bible about his disciples' eyes and ears being blessed (Mt 13:16) are perhaps not at all inclined to settle the dispute, since such a dispute is not a true one and since both ways of participating in the world and being in dialogue have the same origin and together make for the one encounter with the world and indicate the presence of the holy mystery. They might simply say in the words of Angelus Silesius (*Cherubinic Wanderer*, V, 351): "The senses in the spirit are *one* sense for use; whoever looks at God does taste, feel, smell, and hear him, too."

But is it really true that people today have transformed from those of ears and words into those of eyes and images? It is certainly possible that "epochal" changes occur in the way people perceive the ultimate. One can think of the Old Testament, where people had a book about God but were not allowed to make an image of God. However, this frequently bemoaned change today can be much more easily explained, provided it really exists. One could say that the modern sciences in their almost unlimited specializations, their masses of books, their abstract statements, their "demythologizing" of theology (which is always a debunking of the image, however important such demythologizing may be), and their abundance of words have increased immensely in recent years, much more so than the visual, so that today's hunger for the image is ultimately a justified attempt to preserve a balance between hearing and seeing. While it is sad and disturbing that next to the empty talk we now seem to have a limitless supply of the "empty" picture, it is not surprising. After all, people are born to see and invited to behold. They can and have to learn to see in ever new ways, namely, with the concentrated gaze that allows the images to come into full flower, pure and as if freshly born from mystery. These images can be of undemanding simplicity and beauty or they can be images, such as that of the crucified one, that bring to light out of the dark depth of our fate that which is incomprehensible, inevitable—images, in short, that God has created or that we have created for

God. And since seeing is truly human work, more so than "submissive" hearing, people are seen by the way they see; they unmask themselves and reveal much about themselves by how they see and by what images they create. According to the scriptures, one can see in a person's eye that person's fear, nostalgia, pride, compassion, mercy, malice, envy, contempt, jealousy, or deceit. By seeing we make ourselves and we shape ourselves.

But we need to learn to see. People need not only make the "effort at defining," as Hegel puts it, but also the effort at seeing because they have received this gift of grace. When the greatest speech is the one made shortly before one falls silent; when people can learn to be silent most easily by seeing; when we Christians look for the "appearance of God" in confessing Christ both as the image (2 Cor 4:4) and the word of God, then it is a high calling and a holy, human, and Christian art to learn how to see. We simply think that we know how to do it and that nothing could be easier than that. To borrow from scripture that says "Let those who have eyes, see," one could perhaps also say, "Only those who have learned to see (with the eyes of love) will be blessed." Those who have learned to see with a "simple eye" (Mt 6:22) have the true "worldview."

A PRAYER FOR HOPE

We pray, God of grace and eternal life, that you may increase in us and strengthen in us hope. Grant us this virtue of the strong, this power of the confident, this courage of the unshaken. Let us always have a longing for you who are the infinite fulfillment of our life, let us always count on you and your faithfulness, let us always unflinchingly hold onto your power, let us be of such a mind, shape in us such a mind by your Holy Spirit, for then, our Lord and God, will we have the virtue of hope. Then we can tackle the task of our life with courage, then there will live in us the joyous confidence of not laboring in vain, then we will do our work knowing that you the Almighty One are at work in us and through us and, wherever our strength fails, without us for your glory and to our salvation in the ways you see fit. Strengthen in us your hope.

But the true hope of glory, eternal God, is your only begotten Son. He is the one possessing your eternal nature from eternity to eternity because you gave it to him and continue to do so, in eternal creation, so that he owns everything that we hope and long for; he is wisdom and power, beauty and goodness, life and glory, everything in all. And he, this your Son to whom you have given everything, he has become one of us. He became human. Your eternal word, God of Glory, has become flesh, has become like one of us, has lowered himself and accepted human form, a human body, a human soul, a human life, a human fate all the way to its most terrible possibilities. Your son, Holy Father, has truly become human. In adoration we bend our knee. For who can conceive of the incomprehensibility of your love? You loved the world so much that people still take offense at your love and call the message about your son's becoming human foolishness and nonsense. Yet, we believe in this incomprehensibility, the burning courage of your love. And because we believe, we can rejoice in blessed hope: Christ in us is the hope of glory. For when you give us your son, what else could there be that you are holding back, what else could you be refusing? When we possess your son, to whom you have given everything, including your own nature, what could still be lacking? And he is truly ours. For he is the son of Mary, who in Adam is our sister; he is a child of the family of Adam, he is one nature with us, he is of the same being and origin as humans. And when we humans are to form one great community by virtue of our nature and destiny according to your plan and your creator's will, then we share as poor children of Eve's the nature and the destiny of your own son. We are brothers of the firstborn, the only begotten, brothers of your son, heirs in his glory. We participate in his mercy, in his spirit, in his life, in his destiny of cross and glory, in his eternal majesty. No longer do we live our life, but Christ, our brother does, who lives his life in us and through us. Look at us, Father of Jesus Christ and our father, and see that we are prepared to participate in the life of your son. Transform our life and make it resemble the life of your son. He wishes to continue to live his life in us until the end of time; he wants to reveal in us and in our life the majesty, the greatness, the beauty, and the salvific power of his life. What we encounter in life is not coincidence, not blind destiny, but a piece of the life of your son. We want to receive joy as the joy of Christ, success as his success, pain as his pain, suffering as his suffering, work as his work, death as participation in his death.

Consequently, we pray especially for your grace to allow us to take part in the life of Jesus. Allow us to participate in Jesus as the one who is praying. He is the great worshiper of God in spirit and in truth; he is the mediator through whom alone our prayer can penetrate to the throne of grace. In him we want to pray, united by his prayer. He, with whom we are one in spirit, has taught us to pray. He taught us to pray the way he himself prayed: praying at all times and not giving up, praying persistently, confidently, humbly, in spirit and in truth, in genuine love of one's neighbor without which no prayer before you can ever be pleasing. May he teach us to pray for what he prayed for: that your name be glorified, that your will be done, that your kingdom come, for when we pray like that for the sake of your honor, then you will also hear us when we are praying for ourselves, our earthly well-being, help with our earthly sorrows. Grant us the spirit of prayer, of collectedness, and of union with you.

Lord, take my poor heart. It is often so far from you. It is like waterless, dry land, lost in a thousand things and in the trifles that fill up my everyday life. Lord, only you can collect the thoughts of my heart and have it concentrate on you, you who are the center of all hearts, the Lord of all souls. Only you can bestow the spirit of prayer, only your grace is able to allow me to find you amidst this multitude of things, amidst the distractions of everyday life, you, the one necessity, the one person with whom my heart can become still. May your spirit assist me in my weakness, and when I do not know for what I should be praying, then may the spirit intercede for me with groaning too deep for words, and you as the one who knows hearts will listen to what your spirit in me desires when making its intercession.

Finally, I pray for the most difficult and hardest thing: for the grace to recognize the suffering of my life as the cross of your son, to worship in him your holy, unsearchable will, to follow your son on his walk with the cross for as long as it may please you. Allow me to become sensitive to *your* glory and not merely my own well-being, for then I will be able to carry many a cross as the penance for my sins. Do not allow me to become bitter on account of suffering, but rather help me to become mature, patient, selfless, mild, and full of longing for the country in which there is no sorrow and for the day when you will wipe away every tear from the eyes of those who have loved you and who, while in pain and darkness, have believed in your love and your light. Allow my suffering to be a confession of my faith in your promises, a confession of my hope in your mercy and faithfulness, a confession of my love to show that I love you more than myself, that I love for your sake without gain. May the cross of my Lord be an example to me, a strength to me, a solace to me, the solution to all hidden doubt, the light of all nights.

Grant that we may glory in the cross of our Lord Jesus Christ; grant that we may become so mature in true Christian stature and life that we will no longer consider the cross as a disaster and an unintelligible contradiction but as the sign of your choosing us, as the secret and certain sign that we belong to you for all eternity. Your word is faithful and says that when we allow ourselves to die with him, we will also live with him; when we persevere with him, we will also reign with him. Lord, we want to share everything with your son, his life, his divine glory and, hence, also his pain and his death. Only grant us along with the cross the strength to carry it. Allow us to experience also the blessing of the cross, and place on our shoulders that cross which in your wisdom you see as being to our salvation and not to our demise.

Son of the Father, Christ, you who are living in us, you are the hope of our glory. Live in us, subject our life to the norms of your life, make our life like yours. Live in me, pray in me, suffer in me, for no more than that do I ask. For when I have you, I am rich. Those who have found you have found the strength and victory for their life. Amen.

A THEOLOGY OF EVERYDAY LIFE

THEOLOGICAL MEDITATIONS
ON EVERYDAY THINGS

If your everyday life seems poor to you, don't accuse it;
accuse yourself because you have not been strong enough to
call up its riches.

—*Rainer Maria Rilke*

Overwhelmed by the busyness and haste and activity of daily life, many people will read theological meditations such as these only on Sundays, when there is peace and time for reflection. Could we use Sunday, which is like the proverbial catching of one's breath from daily life, to take the opportunity to do some meditating about a theology of everyday life, of such daily activities as work and leisure, eating and sleeping and the like, and place them under the light of the Christian faith and consider them in terms of theology? This, of course, is to be done with the caveat that one cannot say very much in brevity even about such simple things, especially since the simplest things tend to be in truth the most difficult both in theory and in practice.

At this point only very brief points will be offered by way of introduction about a theology of everyday life. The first point is this: Such a theology must not assume it should elevate the everyday to a feast day. Let it be the everyday, such a theology says. The fact is that one cannot and should not try to convert the everyday into a Sunday by means of the lofty thoughts of faith and the wisdom of eternity. One has to live in it in an unsweetened and matter-of-fact way. Then it is exactly what it is meant to be for the Christian: the place of faith, the school of matter-of-factness, the exercise of patience, the wholesome unmasking of big words and of false ideals, the quiet possibility to love truly and faithfully, the space for objectivity, which is the seed of ultimate wisdom.

The second point is this: The simple and honestly accepted everyday life contains in itself the eternal and the silent mystery, which we call God and his secret grace, especially when this life remains the everyday. Because, after all, it is the everyday work that humans do. Wherever people are, there they are creatures who unlock the hidden depths of reality in their free, responsible actions. Even the most common small things are in truth (or should be) inserted as an expression of an interior trait of existence into a truly human life, a life that has the imprint of the eternal God by whom it is grasped and toward whom it is oriented in all of its most serious expressions of freedom through faith, hope, and love. To love God is first and foremost shown not by our ideals, our lofty words, our introspection, but by the act that rips selfishness away from us; by caring, through which we forget ourselves on account of the other; by patience, which makes us silent and wise. People who place their small time into the heart of eternity, which they already carry within, will suddenly realize that even small things have inexpressible depths, are messengers of eternity, are always more than they appear to be, are like drops of water in which is reflected the entire sky, like signs pointing beyond themselves, like messengers running ahead of the message they are carrying and announcing the coming of eternity, like shadows of true reality that are cast over us because the real is already very near.

And, therefore, there is a third point: One should be good to small things—the things of everyday life that are the modest and insignificant—and treat them in a Sunday-like manner. They are irritating only when we receive them in an irritated way; they are boring only when we don't understand them for what they are; they make us ordinary and common only when we don't interpret them correctly and treat them the wrong way. They make us sober, perhaps tired and disappointed, humble and quiet. But that is exactly what we are supposed to become, what is difficult to learn and yet has to be learned, what will ultimately prepare us to face the true festival of eternal life, which God's grace bestows on us, not we ourselves. They need not make us bitter and cynical. After all, the small is the revelation of the great, and this present time is the maturing of eternity. That is true for everyday life as well as for Sundays.

About Work

Work is the characteristic content of what we call our workday and everyday life. One can certainly sing the praises of the wonders of work and mean by that the act of elevated and powerful human creativity, thereby bestowing a blessing on the activity of work. One can also abuse work (how often this happens!) by using it as an escape from self, from the mystery and the question of existence, from fear, which prompts one to look for security. But the true meaning of work lies somewhere in the middle. It is neither an elevated act nor the analgesic of existence. Work is simply that: work. It is tedious while still bearable, average and habitual, steadily repetitive, sustaining one's livelihood and wearing out one's life, inevitable and (when it does not lead to bitter cynicism) perhaps even pleasant. It can never be completely "suitable"; even when it starts out as the highest creative human impulse, work eventually becomes the inevitable humdrum, the gray tedium of repetition, the effort to exert dominance over the unprecedented, and the painful burden of doing not what springs from internal motivation but what is imposed from the outside and by the other. And always work is also having to fit into the demands of others, into the rhythm that is given, a contribution to a common goal that no one has individually selected, hence an obedience and a renunciation for the sake of the everyday.

The first thing a theology of work has to say is that work remains and ever will be just that: work—the laborious monotony, the demand for self-renunciation, the everyday. Work may contain elements of creativity, but it remains tied to a biological basis that seeks its fulfillment in death, remaining always in a symbiosis with the outer world that can never be completely controlled. Therefore, it inevitably remains work and that is what scripture says of it: Work is the manifestation of an existence governed by guilt, a disharmony in our life between internal and external, freedom and necessity, body and spirit, individual and society that can find resolution only through God. But this manifestation of guilt, which is a consequence but not guilt itself, has become also the manifestation of bodily deliverance in Christ. And this is true not only for death, the most radical manifestation of guilt, but for all things that evidence a distancing from God. It is true for work that is painful, ordinary, and self-giving. Not on our own but only by the grace of Christ can work become as "done unto the Lord," an exercise in the attitude and orientation that enable God to infuse it with the joy of eternal life: patience (which is the image of faith in everyday life), faithfulness, objectivity, responsibility, selflessness, and love.

About Walking

One of the most common things in daily life is walking. We realize this when we can no longer walk because we are imprisoned, for example, or lame. Then, we suddenly recognize the ability to walk as a grace and a miracle. We are not plants tied to a specific locale destined by nature, but we choose our environment, we change it, we select it, we walk. While walking, we experience ourselves as those who are changing, as those who are searching, as those who have yet to arrive. We realize that we are the ones walking toward a goal and not simply drifting toward nothingness. Also, by walking toward that which is difficult and cannot be avoided we experience ourselves as those who are free, provided that despite the burden we are still allowed to walk toward that goal. We talk about a walk of life, and it is worth noting that the name first given to Christians was "people of the way" (Acts 9:2). If we want to say that we are not just listeners but also doers of the word, then scripture tells that we need to not only live in the spirit but also walk in it. We talk about the proceeding of happenings, the good outcome of an undertaking, the access to knowledge and insight, someone's devious going behind another's back, an event as a process, change as a transition, the end as a going down. And we conceive of becoming as an ascent, our life as a pilgrimage, history as progress, what is clear as accessible, a decision as a step. Among the elements of a great festival—in both religious and secular life—are the procession and the parade. Even such small and sparse examples show that we interpret our entire life along the lines of a very basic, fundamental experience, namely that of ordinary walking.

We walk. And by this simple physical act we are saying that we do not have a resting place, that we are on the way, that we have yet to arrive, that we are still searching for the goal and are pilgrims, wanderers between two worlds, people in transition, moved and moving, steering the imposed movement while experiencing through our deliberate movement that we do not always arrive where we had planned to go. In the simplicity of walking, which always involves knowledge and freedom, the entirety of human existence is actually summed up and brought to the fore; it is the "being here," the destination of which is revealed by the faith of the Christian and in which arrival is promised. Thus, existence is an eternal motion, in which a person is aware of walking and of not yet having arrived; both a searching and a believing that one will find because (and here we cannot put it any differently) God himself is coming down and back as Lord, as the one who is our future.

We walk and we are compelled to search. But the ultimate, the essential, walks toward us, searches for us, yet does so only when we are the ones walking also, walking toward it. And when we have found because we *were* found, we will know that our walking was supported (the being supported is called grace) by the power of that movement that comes toward us, namely the moving toward us of God.

About Sitting Down

Sitting belongs to everyday life and therefore also in a theology about it. Who has not experienced sitting down with gratitude and gladness after some exhausting work or a hiking trip? Who does not have the wish, in spite of restless longings, to finally settle down? Who does not know that one will have to really sit down if a project is to succeed and have worth? To sit down means from a biological and secular perspective that not all places and circumstances are of equal value, that people belong somewhere and cannot be equally at home everywhere, that they finally want to rest, so that all movement can only be pointing toward one's homeland, where one settles as the final place of one's true and fulfilled life.

Such sitting down in the physical sense can, of course, express only one side of human existence and its fulfillment. While not negating it, the term does not explicitly say that the peace of fulfillment, the having arrived at the place where one finally settles, will also be the place of eternal life, completed activity, the absolute experience of a most vibrant reality. Yet, this is exactly what happens while at rest, during gathered stillness, in a gladly restful state of permanence, without fear of loss, without disquietude and empty activity; it happens while at rest, while sitting down, just as in the scriptures that speak of the banquet of eternal life: And the Lord will allow them to sit down (Lk 12:37). All of this sounds rather peaceful and harmless. But behind it hide some serious questions for us: Do we have the courage, the discipline, and the freedom of heart to be quiet, to sit down? Do we become immediately bored when we have to sit down quietly and, while driving or traveling, throw ourselves into constant activity because we cannot endure ourselves, the quiet and the silence? Do we always have to be on the run because we are running away from ourselves? Can we experience Sunday only as a form of an altered workday, as a physically imposed pause amidst the activity of everyday life?

We need to learn that inactivity can be and ultimately is a higher form of activity, namely that of the heart, which serves the person as a whole. From personal experience we have to understand that by driving fast we are not excused from having to know where we plan on going; also, that someone who is going slowly often arrives faster by first carefully considering the destination and the best route to take. The infinite movement inherent in the destination (if one may be permitted to speak in paradox) is more than dead resting. But we are still on the way to that movement, and we reach it only by choosing to rest as opposed to what looks better and more comfortable, namely an empty activity that comes from wanting to flee from ourselves.

Of course, there are many exercises that lead to quiet and silent resting in oneself, such as the experience of a true object of art and of pure music, of deep and pure love between two people, of enlightened insight and knowledge not aimed at utility, as well as other experiences related to the arts, the humanities, and contemplation. Ultimately, however, there is only one type of stillness that enables a person to be at peace with himself or herself: prayer (regardless of the term one may use for it). Only in the loving being-at-oneness with the infinite mystery we call God can one arrive in such a way that one does not have to go any farther, where one can find rest (which is not just a moment amidst scurrying activity), where one can hear the word for which all sitting down and resting is only an analogy and a promise: whoever prevails I will allow to sit down with me on my throne (Rev 3:21).

About Seeing

Among the most fundamental and basic human functions in everyday life is seeing. We conceive of seeing—regardless of whether it is physiological or epistemological—as the most objective and concrete way of relating to the world in which we live. Seeing opens up for us the widest reach of the world; it brings up close what is far away and distinguishes between the close-by and us. It organizes, differentiates, and connects things, shaping one world that is diverse and beautiful. But the eye is also (just as in scripture) the window that one steps up to and through which one is seen, the gate by which not only does the human world enter into the person but also the person steps out of the hidden interior and is revealed. According to scripture, the eye reveals a person's fear, longing, pride, pity, mercy, malice, jealousy, ridicule, envy, and falsehood. Scripture also uses the image of the eye to describe what lies outside a person, the exterior that one looks at, whereas God looks at the heart, a person's interior deliberate inaccessibility, a person's very core. Thus the eye that sees and searches becomes the mysterious middle between the human being and the world, the interior and the exterior, between gathering and giving away, revealing and concealing. It would make things too complex and lengthy to say more here about how religious language has used the activity of seeing in relation to hearing, the problem of their incongruence and their congruence, as an expression of an encounter with God and Christ. Let us stay with the role of seeing in everyday life. For here also can the activity of seeing say something about who one is or should be: the open one, the circumspect one, the one inclined toward what is distant and elusive, the one with the courage and the innocence to become transparent, letting the interior show, giving expression to it, and being willing to live with the fact that one is known the way one is. Whoever looks at the world and at oneself like that or, in other words, dares to see the world the way it is without adding another layer, imposing upon the simple image an ideal; whoever shows what one truly is without inserting a second image that separates reality from appearances, sees simply and has spiritual eyes that are healthy. To that person, the saying from Jesus' Sermon on the Mount applies when everyday seeing with the eye is an image and a parable of what it means to have the proper perspective on life: The light of your body is the eye. When your eye is simple, your entire body will be full of light (Mt 6:22).

About Laughter

One would hope that part of everyday life is not just the seriousness of everyday work but also laugher. Laughter is a very serious matter, because it can reveal more about a person than words can. In talking here about laughter, we mean good laughter. Yes, there is also the laughter of fools and sinners, according to the wise Ben Sira (Sir 21:20; 27:13), a laughter that draws the Lord's curse (Lk 6:25). That is not what we are talking about. We mean here the liberating laughter that springs from a childlike and joyous heart. It can live only in a person who is kindly disposed toward the world and toward people and has an open and relaxed sympathy, which can take anything and see anything the way it is: the great as great, the small as small, the serious as serious, and the ridiculous as something to laugh about. Since all of this exists and God has meant for it to exist, it should be accepted the way it is and not as all the same; this means we need to laugh about the comical and ridiculous. But people can do so only when they do not associate everything with themselves, when they are free of themselves, having sympathy with everything and all and allowing things and people to have a voice. Only loving people have such sympathy. Therefore, good laughter is a sign of love, a revelation and a school of the love of everything in God.

Still, the innocuous, innocent laughter of the children of God is even more, for it is an analogy. Scripture itself depicts laughter, this small creature that one might assume would quietly dissolve into nothingness upon entering the halls of God's eternity, as the image and illustration of God's disposition. Scripture could tell us something frightening about God, but instead says that God up there is laughing, laughing the laughter of someone who is carefree, confident, and not threatened; laughing the laughter of divine sovereignty in light of all the gruesome chaos of a blood-filled, torturous, and madly mean world history; laughing in a relaxed manner, almost, one might say, unshaken, sympathetic, and aware of the tear-filled spectacle of this earth. God can do so because his eternal word has already cried with and suffered this world's utter God-forsakenness. God laughs, scripture says, showing that even in the remotest laughter springing up somewhere clear and pure from a good heart over some stupidity of the world, there also lights up an image and reflection of God, an image of the victorious, the glorious God of history and eternity, whose own laughter attests to the fact that ultimately everything will be well.

About Eating

Our constant talking and writing about the chemical and physiological aspects of eating put us at risk of seeing this activity, which is part of everyday life and yet so mysterious, as merely a type of charging up on physical energy in order to keep our bodily machine running. Yet, when a person really eats, rather than taking in food like an animal, eating becomes a matter that involves the entire person. Consequently, when the aspect of eating as involving the entire person is lost, the physiological side of eating suffers.

There is hardly anything more mysterious in everyday life than nourishment: the transformation of something dead into something alive, the acceptance of something that is other as one's own, the adopting of something into a higher and more comprehensive reality while its own nature is being preserved.

Those who think life is only a mechanically complicated construct of a mere chemical and physical reality cannot marvel at this process of transformation. In human beings, such a transformation moves toward what is human, toward a reality that has come into its own, is at home with itself, disposes of itself, and can offer a home to the world. If one says that the lower can be understood only from the perspective of the higher (and not the other way around, as a dull thinker might presume), then one has to say also that eating is the lowest, yet the most basic form of a process that goes like this: A being consciously accepts what is outside and in the world and lovingly surrenders to the entirety of the world. It is therefore quite logical that when one tries to explain a greater and higher form of human existence in its whole, concrete bodily form, one prefers to use the meal as a symbol. But this symbol is also tangible reality in the loving and trusting unity of those who eat, because they allow one another access to the common ground of their existence, bodily nourishment, and in giving of themselves, they communicate with one another. Thus, the meal becomes a symbol of ultimate human unity, finding its fulfillment when all are sharing in the meal of eternity that makes for union with God and with one another, when they are eating the one bread and drinking the one cup, which is the Lord himself. Regardless of where we eat, there still should be something festive about the everyday meal, for it is the banquet of the everyday. It announces the unity that everything and everyone longs for, where all are led to safety and delivered from their loneliness, and it speaks in its low yet audible voice amidst everyday life of the banquet of life eternal.

About Sleeping

We sleep away a good third of our lives. Hence, sleep belongs very much to our everyday life as an activity and art form that all are able to engage in and practice.

Is there such a thing as a theology of sleeping? Most certainly there is. In a wonderfully earthy way, scripture first of all confirms our own experience with sleep: It talks about the solid sleep of the one who has worked hard, the destructive sleeplessness of the one in charge of many things, the excessive sleep of the lazy one, and similar things. But scripture also sees in sleep an image and reflection of a deeper reality of human existence: the image of death, the image of dead and deadening dullness, the image of being mired in sin. Also, scripture sees in sleep an inner relaxation, where a person is receptive to the instructions of God (as if given by the Lord in one's sleep), a time for meaningful dreams that can clarify God's directions and call and that can perhaps make one conscious of what is otherwise repressed.

Yes indeed, everyday sleep is something very mysterious. People are individual and free, autonomous and self-directed; but when sleeping, they surrender, let go, entrust themselves to the powers of their existence that they themselves did not create and cannot oversee. Sleep is an act of trusting one's deepest inner conviction, one's own certainty, and the goodness of the human world. It is an act of innocence and of consenting to the elusive. If one approached sleep like that, not as a merely dull succumbing to physiological mechanisms but as an agreeable and trusting acceptance of an utterly human act, then falling asleep could be seen as relating to the inner structure of prayer, which is equally a letting-go, an entrusting of one's own inner conviction to the providence of God which one lovingly accepts. It is small wonder that a Christian has the impression that sleep should be preceded by evening prayer which, depending on the one praying, must be a willing, cleansing, and conciliatory saying goodbye to the day and its everyday life and an entrusting of oneself to the mystery that always lovingly envelops us. By welcoming sleep in a prayerful way, one also bestows a blessing upon the dark depth of one's own being where sleep takes us. And the angels of God, not those of the dark deep, will be guarding our sleep.

Then sleep is peaceful and relaxed, a communication with the depth in which needs to be grounded and rooted whatever makes us free as human beings, all conscious planning of life, if we want to remain whole or wish to be.

About the Experience of Grace in Everyday Life

Have you ever had the experience of grace? By that we do not mean some pious sentiment, a holiday-type religious emotion, a subtle feeling of relief, but simply the experience of grace: being overcome by the Holy Spirit of the Trinitarian God, which has become a reality in Christ through his becoming human and his sacrifice on the cross.

Can one even experience grace in this life? Would answering "yes" not destroy the faith, this clear-dark cloud that envelops us as long as we are pilgrims here? It is true that the mystics say—and they would back up the truth of their statement with the sacrifice of their life—that they have experienced God and hence grace. But the experiential knowledge of God in mysticism is a dark and mysterious subject matter: one cannot talk about it when one has not had the experience and one *will* not talk about it when one has. This means we cannot answer this question so readily. Perhaps there are grades of the experience of grace, of which at least the lowest is accessible to us.

Let us ask ourselves first: Have we ever experienced the spiritual dimension of humans? (What is meant here by "spiritual" is another difficult question that cannot be quickly answered.) We might say: Of course I have had this experience; I have it daily and I always have. I think, I study, I make decisions, I act, I cultivate relationships with other people, I live in a society that is not merely based on the concrete but also on the spiritual, I love, I am glad, I read poetry, I enjoy culture's goods of science, the arts, and so on, which is to say, I know what spirit is.

But things are not quite that simple. While what has been said is true, the way in which "spirit" is (or could be) interpreted here is only as a type of ingredient used to make earthly life human, beautiful, and somewhat meaningful. The spirit in its true transcendence may not necessarily have been experienced here. This does not mean that spirit exists only where one talks and philosophizes about spirit in its transcendence. On the contrary, for then it would be only a deduced and second-hand experience of that spirit which is not limited to being at work only as an inward moment in human life.

Where then is there a true experience of spirit? About that we want to say first: Let us try to discover the spirit in our own experience. One can point here only in a tentative and rather cautious manner to one or the other thing.

Have we ever remained silent even though we wished to defend ourselves, even though we had been treated unjustly? Have we ever forgiven, even though we did not get rewarded for it and the quiet act of forgiveness was taken for granted? Have we ever been obedient, not because we had to and wanted to avoid negative consequences, but purely on account of the mysterious, silent, incomprehensible one we call God and his will? Have we ever sacrificed without a thank-you, without recognition, even without a sense of inner satisfaction? Have we ever been utterly alone? Have we ever made a decision based solely on the deepest voice of our conscience, the place where one cannot talk to anyone, cannot make things clear to anyone, where one is totally alone and knows one is making a decision that will not be accepted by a single person and for which one will have to pay from here on out? Have we ever tried to love God when we were no longer carried by a wave of passionate excitement, when we could no longer confuse our own self and our drive in life with God, when it seemed we would die of such love and when it resembled death and total negation, when we felt as if we were calling out to a void and to utter unresponsiveness, when we appeared to be faced with making a terrible jump into an abyss, when everything seemed elusive and meaningless? Have we ever done our duty in a way that carried with it the burning sensation that we were utterly betraying our convictions and canceling ourselves out by apparently committing a terrible blunder, by doing what no one would thank us for? Have we ever been good to someone and received no word of gratitude, no acknowledgment, not even the reward of being recognized as having acted selflessly, or fairly, or kindly?

Let us search our lives to see if we have ever known such things. When we find them, we will recognize that we have experienced the spirit that we are talking about. The experience of eternity, the experience that spirit is more than a piece of this temporal world, the experience that the purpose of being human does not rise and fall with the meaning and happiness of this world, the experience of courage and of a faith that risks a leap, a faith not supported by reason or derived from the world's principles of success.

From that we can understand the secret passion that resides in people of the spirit and in the saints. They *want* to have this experience. Forever driven by the hidden fear of becoming stuck in the world, they want to reassure themselves and so they begin living in the spirit. They develop a taste for the spirit. While the average person considers such experiences as unpleasant though not entirely unavoidable interruptions of the normal course of life and views spirit as merely the spice and decorative flavor of a different life but not life's essential ingredient, people of the spirit and the saints have tasted the flavor of pure spirit. They drink it pure, so to speak, and do not merely enjoy it as the spice of earthly existence. It is the reason for their strange way of life, their poverty, their desire for humility, their longing for death, their willingness to suffer, their secret longing for martyrdom. Not that they do not have weaknesses. Not that they have no need to be always returning to the ordinariness of the everyday. Not that they do not know that grace can also bless everyday life and thoughtful activity and can transform each action into a step toward God. Not that they do not know that we are no angels and should not wish to be. But they know that the human being is supposed to live as spirit in concrete human existence, not merely in speculative thought but truly at the border between God and world, time and eternity. And they continually try to make sure that they are actually doing so, that the spirit within them does not just become a means that facilitates human existence.

And now, when we have had this experience of the spirit, then we (at least we Christians who live by faith) have factually experienced the supernatural. Perhaps it was in a rather anonymous way and not explicit. Perhaps it was in a way in which we were not able to turn around, not allowed to turn around to look at the supernatural directly. But we know that when we surrender ourselves to the experience of the spirit, when the graspable and observable and the enjoyable recede, when everything sounds like deathly silence, when everything takes on the flavor of death and perdition, when everything seems to dissolve into an inexpressible sense of blessedness that is at once white and colorless and elusive, then we are experiencing not only spirit but the Holy Spirit at work. Then the hour of the Spirit's grace has come. Then there is the seemingly ominous abyss of God, who communicates himself to us in the dawn of the arrival of his eternity, which no longer has streets, which has the taste of nothingness because it is eternity. When we have let go and no longer are in possession of ourselves, when we have renounced ourselves and no longer have the upper hand, when everything and we ourselves have been transported an infinite distance from ourselves, then we are beginning to live in the world of God, the God of grace and eternal life. Initially, this might seem strange to us, and we will be ever tempted to flee in fright into the familiar and the near, and we will have to do so and will be allowed to do so frequently. But gradually we should try to get accustomed to the taste of the pure wine of the spirit that is filled with Holy Spirit, at least to the point where we no longer reject the cup handed to us by his leading and providence.

In this life, the cup of the Holy Spirit is identical to the cup of Christ. But those who will drink from it are only those who have slowly begun to taste in emptiness the fullness, in descent the ascent, in death life, in giving up gain. Those who learn to do so have the experience of the spirit, of pure spirit, and, with that, the experience of the Holy Spirit of grace. For this setting-free of the spirit can occur largely and in the long run only by Christ's mercy through faith. Wherever he sets free the spirit, he does so by supernatural grace for the sake of life with God.

Let us look for the experience of grace in our life. That is not so that we can say: here it is, I have it. One cannot find grace and then triumphantly advertise it as one's possession and property. One can look for it only by forgetting about it; one can find it only by looking for God and giving oneself to God in self-forgetful love without going back to self. But we should also ask sometimes whether there lives in us something of this death-dealing and life-infusing experience in order to determine how far we have yet to go and how far away we still are from the experience of the Holy Spirit in our so-called spiritual life. *Grandis nobis restat via. Venite et gustate, quam suavis sit Dominus!* A long path lies ahead of us. Come and taste how good is the Lord!

WORDS FOR THE START OF THE DAY

In God's Name

We are beginning a new day. Yes, it is bound to bring the same old strain and the same old burden. It will run in a murky and ordinary fashion through our life and disappear in ordinary fashion the same way it is arriving now that we are facing it: gray and unattractive. Let us join in the old Christian saying: in God's name. The new day is coming in God's name, conceived of by wisdom and love. It presents the opportunity to do one's duty in patient loyalty, the opportunity given to us by God to have it be the field of time on which, amidst toil, the fruit of eternity is meant to mature. Let us say courageously and even cheerfully and with confidence: in God's name. In the name of the strong God, who is the quiet strength of the weak. In the name of the holy God, who by his Holy Spirit can make radiant and imbue with grace the small things of common duty so that they become big things of holy and eternal value. In the name of the merciful God, who desires that our peace, our patience, our friendliness, and our trusting good-will give evidence of the fact that at the heart of all reality is God himself, holy grace and eternal love. Let us say openly and from the heart: in the name of God, so that even what is entangled may remain integrated in God's design, so that what is without exit may retain still an open gate to his eternal freedom, so that our tears may be shed in the ultimate peace of God and our laughter may ring all the way into his love. In God's name. May all be done in his name, in Christ's name, both great and small done according to the apostle's injunction: Whatever you do in word or deed, do it all in the name of the Lord Jesus Christ. How good this day would look later this evening if right now we were to say not only verbally and superficially but from the bottom of a faithful, courageous heart: In God's name I am beginning this day.

Each Day Is Unique

We are beginning a new day. The Christian knows: God has given it to me. It is a precious gift, with an unspeakable, mysterious value. Other gifts may be great, but there is hardly one to be found—other than God himself and his love—that could not be replaced by another of equal value. Still, when it comes to time, the moment, the hour, and the day, one cannot replace one time period with another. Each day is unique and irreplaceable. Thus, a strange thing is true: the most fleeting gift of God is, precisely due to its momentary character, also the most precious one, and because it is the most precious one it is also the most vulnerable gift. From a secular perspective, it is possible to postpone until tomorrow what one should do today; from a secular perspective, there may be open space tomorrow for the things of today. But with God it is different: one has to fill today with its designated contents because tomorrow has its own tasks that will use it up in full. Each day is a unique offer, a demanding offer: What you can do today before God in his love, you cannot postpone until tomorrow, for tomorrow God gives you a new task, just as he then gives you a new day. The new task may resemble the old like one egg the other, yet it is completely new, completely different, just like the unique today and the unique tomorrow are different, like no day can return with the next but is given only once, never to return. This unrelenting uniqueness is not only the pain of time but also its nobility and a reflection of the divine, unique eternal. Therefore, let us today give this unique day its divine content: love, peace, patience, loyalty, courage, and cheerful hope. When that happens, this day becomes a full day, a truly unique, irreplaceable day. And the fleeting gift of passing time bears the fruit of eternity.

Life Is Eternally Open

We are beginning a new day. Perhaps we have the impression that it only perpetuates the old pain and that it drags into the future the burden of the past. This is true: upon the house of the present are pressing the mortgage dues of the past, and our future is in many respects the past that has become big and fully grown. One can no longer simply undo the past in all of its aspects. Life is no experiment that one can repeat at leisure. And still: In the most ultimate and deepest sense, one can always start completely new, completely from the beginning, freshly gleaming like the first day. The priest, even the old one who already has his life behind him, a life that can no longer be changed, prays each morning: I want to approach the altar of God, want to approach God, who renews my youth. He is right. We have missed many chances, squandered many opportunities, will not be able to return to a crossroad and take a different path. But when the highest and most comprehensive opportunity—and its name is God—still lies before us, when the greatest chance—which is his love—is still being offered, when the point at which we stand still is an open path to him, and that is the case, then it is true: then nothing is actually truly squandered or lost. Then life remains open, the blessedly dangerous risk of the true and real life that matters most, and it remains to be filled with all of its promises. Then one can forget what lies in the past, then one can start anew as if nothing had happened, then nothing of eternal value is really lost. The new beginning may look ridiculously small and meager: a little more cheeriness, a little more attention paid to others and their pain, a little more patience and understanding. But a small resolve to do things like that, such a small beginning, such a new start can be the start of a new life. One realizes suddenly that a life oriented to God is still eternally open. Eternal hope is entering everyday life.

New Day, Be Welcomed!

An old adage says that one should not praise the day before evening. In many ways that is true, of course. But such an adage contains a truth that is not necessarily part of the deepest truths but rather belongs to brief sayings of popular wisdom that do not always contain essential, ultimate truth. Not that one should then scorn such a saying. Jesus, too, loved words of popular wisdom and pithy sayings such as: Each day has enough troubles of its own. But in such words one can also try to see the other side of reality that is easily concealed by them. And therefore, one can also say: Praise the day even before it is evening. Then you do not receive it with distrust and caution, but with the praise of trust, of hope that it will turn into what you can praise in the evening for good reason. Then, the same happens to the day as happens to people, at least to children: they become what one believes them to be. Onward then! Let us praise the day before evening; let us say to it: Be welcomed, Messenger of God, Little Child of the Eternity of our God. Be praised, Little Moment of Time, which arrives for no other reason than to disappear in the evening into the eternity of God. Be praised, Day, where I can pay off a little debt of the heart and of love, which I am given by others; be praised, Little Garden of Time, from which I can harvest faith and love, the fruit of eternity, no matter what; be welcomed with joy, you small poor day: I will turn you into a small work of art, into a blessed, serious play of life, where everything plays a part: God, the world, and my heart. Don't you think

that one is surely allowed to praise the day before the evening
when in the morning one has prayerfully praised it like that
before God?

On the Feast of St. Joseph

Today is the feast of St. Joseph. That should not only be the
occasion for congratulating the many Josephs in our land on
their name's day, not only be the reason for going a little beyond such a customary tradition and including these Josephs
in a heartfelt intercessory prayer before God. The feast of St.
Joseph is one that praises the blessing of the ordinary, the
everyday, that which we are in the process of starting. One
could say: The feast of St. Joseph is a feast of the weekday, a
feast of everyday life. For what can be said of Joseph in terms
of honor and praise is the same that one should also be able to
say about us: that he was a just and loyal person, that for him
deeds were not replaced by words (not a single word of his is
recorded in scripture), that he lived the life of the ordinary
person as one of many, life in a small town, the life of a work-
man, of a political refugee, of a taxpayer, of a man who is mentioned in scripture—the word of God—only where it is unavoidable, so to speak, where something needs to be said about
some of the others, as well, so that even he cannot be completely passed over in silence. And what is said of him? That
he pondered, that he got up and did his duty. And this is said
three times. Without doubt, such things could also be said of
us. Or do we not have the opportunity to practice quiet loyalty, perseverance in the everyday, faith and courage in service
to others? Joseph is a good patron saint and a good role model
not only for the many Josephs among us, but for us all. How
about celebrating, in addition to the church's liturgy, my
everyday life today as a true Joseph's feast, a feast of the God-
filled, God-blessed, and God-guided life of everyday?

On the Feast of St. Benedict

Today, on March 21, we celebrate the feast of St. Benedict. Many of us have seen a Benedictine monk and a monastery of these monks in their black habits, for in today's Austria there are fourteen abbeys for men and two for women; hence, you may have a fair idea that these Benedictines have been named after this Benedict, whose name is printed on the leaf of today's calendar. And many will leave it at that. Still, this Benedict, who died on this day fourteen hundred years ago as abbot of Monte Cassino and who was the father of Western monasticism, is one of the men who by patience and loyalty, by labor, in prayer and self-renunciation, laid the foundation for a new time in an age when the Western world, amidst a dark, seemingly sterile period of decline, was presumed to be only waiting for the end of time with patience and faith in the eternal. Wherever there is even in our time and hence in the situation of our own life a small degree of discipline and order, morality and clarity, mild discretion, and Christian humanism, there continues to live on, though largely concealed, the legacy of Benedict's life. We can be taught by this man of mild inner strength, of discipline and the fear of God, that even in times of dissolution and decay, of addictions and anxieties, one can be a Christian, which means being a person of solid order, of the unity of labor and prayer, of perseverance and hope in the eternal God, who is the lord of all times. To copy Benedict is not possible. But to imitate him is what we all should do. Each Christian family should in our time be something like what his abbeys were in his time: fortresses of fidelity, of labor, of prayer, of quiet perseverance, temples in which the eternal light does not go out, even if it is dark outside, places where time becomes sacred because one lives there for what is eternal.

SOURCES

ADVENT

The Judgment of the Son of Man
Published in the weekly journal *Der Volksbote* 47 (November 24, 1949): 12.

Festival of Faith
Published in *Der Volksbote* 48 (December 1, 1949): 12.

Patience with the Preliminary
Published in *Der Volksbote* 49 (December 8, 1949): 12.

The Trouble with Salvation History
Published in *Der Volksbote* 50 (December 15, 1949): 12.

CHRISTMAS

The Reply of Silence
Published in *Die Presse* (December 22, 1962): 17.

The Great Joy
Published in *Der Volksbote* 51 (December 22, 1949): 1.

Holy Night
First published in *Glaube, der die Erde liebt: Christliche Besinnung im Alltag der Welt*, ed. Karl Lehmann (Freiburg: Herder, 1966), 28–32; published in English as *Everyday Faith*, trans. W. J. O'Hara (New York: Herder and Herder, 1968), 11-13. No records exist in the Karl Rahner archives on where this meditation or sermon was given.

Grace in Human Depths
First version published in the weekly *Die Zeit* 51 (December 21, 1962): 17.

The Arrival of God into a Locked-Up World
First published in *Glaube, der die Erde liebt* (Freiburg: Herder, 1966); in English, *Everyday Faith*, trans. W. J. O'Hara (New York: Herder and Herder, 1968).

NEW YEAR AND EPIPHANY

Spiritual Account of a Year
Published in the monthly journal *Geist und Leben* 30 (1957): 406–8.
In the Name of Jesus
Published in *Der Volksbote* 52 (December 29, 1949): 12.
About the Blessed Journey of Those Looking for God
Published in *Geist und Leben*, 22 (1949): 405–9 and originally titled "Von der seligen Reise des gottsuchenden Menschen: Gedanken zum Fest der Erscheinung des Herrn"; later included in *Kleines Kirchenjahr* (1954) and *Das Große Kirchenjahr* (1987).

LENT

Lent: My Night Knows No Darkness
First published in *Geist und Leben* 21 (1948): 1–5; later published in *Kleines Kirchenjahr* (Munich: Ars Sacra, 1954) and *Das Große Kirchenjahr*, ed. Albert Raffelt (Freiburg: Herder, 1986), the former published in English as *The Eternal Year*, trans. John Shea, S.S. (Baltimore: Helicon Press, 1964), 65-72, the latter as *The Great Church Year*, ed. Albert Raffelt and Harvey Egan, S.J. (New York: Crossroad, 1993), 113–18.

EASTER

The Beginning of Glory
Published in *Der Volksbote* 14 (April 1, 1965): 1.
A Faith that Loves the Earth
Published in *Geist und Leben* 23 (1950): 81–85.

Mysticism of the Earth

Published in *Der Volksbote* 50 (2) 1950: 13; later included in *Das Große Kirchenjahr*, ed. Albert Raffelt (Freiburg: Herder, 1986); published in English as *The Great Church Year*, ed. Albert Raffelt and Harvey Egan, S.J. (New York: Crossroad, 1993).

CORPUS CHRISTI AND PENTECOST

Feast of Daily Bread

Published in *Gottes Wort im Kirchenjahr* (Würzburg: Echter, 1955), 19–21.

Walk with the Lord

Published in *Glaube, der die Erde liebt* (Freiburg: Herder, 1966), 73–76.

Prayer for Pentecost

Published in *Offen sei Dein Herz zur Welt*, ed. Auguste Staud-Weth (Innsbruck: Tyrolia, 1954), 72–74.

LOVE FOR GOD AND NEIGHBOR

The First Commandment

Published in *Der Volksbote* 38 (September 24, 1950): 13.

The New Commission of the One Love

Lecture given at the annual meeting of the Catholic Charity for Girls, Women, and Children, May 11–13, 1965 in Cologne; published in the organization's *Korrespondenzblatt* 35 (1965): 206–16.

Bear with One Another and Forgive Each Other

Sermon preached at the Catholic Conference of the North ("Nordische Katholikentag") on June 18, 1965 in Hamburg; published in *Geist und Leben* 38 (1965) 310–12.

THE ONE SPIRIT—THE MANY GIFTS

Non-Believing Christians and Christian Non-Believers

Published in *Der Volksbote* 3 (January 19, 1950): 12.

People as Prophets and the Church

Published in *Münchener Katholische Kirchenzeitung* 7 (February 15, 1948): 40.

On Not Avoiding Decisions

Published in *Kraft und Ohnmacht: Kirche und Glauben in der Erfahrung unserer Zeit*, ed. Mario von Galli and Manfred Plate (Frankfurt: Knecht, 1963), 84–91.

Christians in the World according to the Church Fathers

Introduction to *Kirchenväter an Laien: Briefe der Seelenführung*, ed. Ludwig von Welsersheimb (Freiburg: Herder, 1939, 1954), 1–17; 5–21.

The Divine Mystery of Marriage

Published in *Geist und Leben* 31 (1958): 107–9.

THE MYSTERY OF THE SAINTS

Feast of Holy Beginnings

Published in the *Korrespondenzblatt* of the *Collegium Canisianum* at Innsbruck, no. 94 (1960): 13–16.

Thomas Aquinas

Published in the *Korrespondenzblatt* of the *Collegium Canisianum* at Innsbruck, no. 95 (1961): 25–28.

Thomas Aquinas as Monk, Theologian, and Mystic

Published in the *Korrespondenzblatt* of the Collegium Canisianum at Innsbruck, no. 86 (1952): 89–93.

Ignatius of Loyola: The Saint's Relevance for Today

Originally published in 1956 as "Der heilige Ignatius und die Englischen Fräulein" on the occasion of the 250th anniversary of the women's order of the English Ladies at St. Pölten, whose founding and charism was inspired by Ignatius of Loyola; this essay was reissued in a slightly edited version in *Geist und Leben* 57 (1984): 337–40.

The Mysticism of Loving All Things in the World according to Ignatius

Lecture given in Vienna and published in *Zeitschrift für Aszese und Mystik* 12 (1937): 121–37.